IV

孫子兵法

Sun Tzu's
Art of War
Playbook
Volume 4 of 9:
Probability

Gary Gagliardi

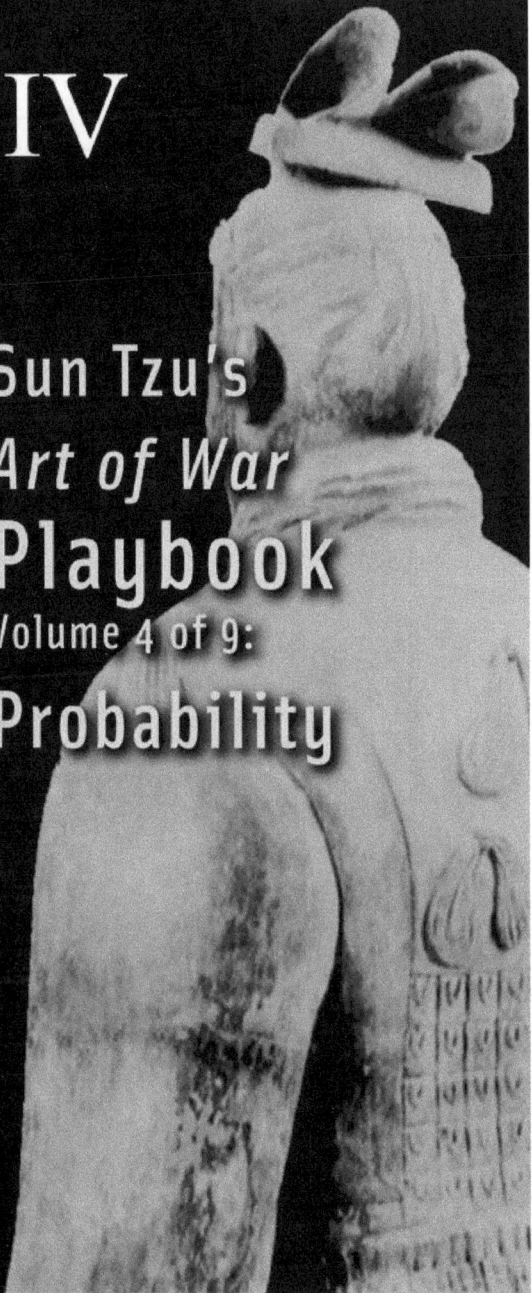

Sun Tzu's Art of War Playbook

Volume Four: Probability

by Gary Gagliardi
The Science of Strategy Institute
Clearbridge Publishing

Published by
Science of Strategy Institute, Clearbridge Publishing
   suntzus.com   scienceofstrategy.org

First Print Edition
Library of Congress Control Number: 2014909969
Also sold as an ebook under the title Sun Tzu's Warrior Playbook
Copyright 2010, 2011, 2012, 2013, 2014 Gary Gagliardi
ISBN 978-1-929194-79-7 (13-digit) 1-929194-79-X (10-digit)

Originally published as a series of articles on the Science of Strategy Website, scienceofstratregy.org. and
later as an ebook on various sites.

PO Box 33772, Seattle, WA 98133
Phone: (206)542-8947 Fax: (206)546-9756
beckyw@clearbridge.com
garyg@scienceofstrategy.org

Manufactured in the United States of America.
Interior and cover graphic design by Dana and Jeff Wincapaw.
Original Chinese calligraphy by Tsai Yung, Green Dragon Arts, www.greendragonarts.com.

Publisher's Cataloging-in-Publication Data
Sun-tzu, 6th cent. B.C.
Strategy, positioning, success, probability
   [Sun-tzu ping fa, English]
   Art of War Playbook / Sun Tzu and Gary Gagliardi.
   p.197 cm. 23
   Includes introduction to basic competitive philosophy of Sun Tzu

Clearbridge Publishing's books may be purchased for business, for any promotional use,
or for special sales.

Contents

Playbook Overview

Note: This overview is provided for those who have not read the previous volume of Sun Tzu's Art of War Playbook. *It provides an brief overview of the work in general and the general concepts framing the first volume.*

Sun Tzu's **The Art of War** is less a "book" in the modern Western sense than it is an outline for a course of study. Like Euclid's Geometry, simply reading the work teaches us very little. Sun Tzu wrote in in a tradition that expected each line and stanza to be studied in the context of previous statements to build up the foundation for understanding later statements.

To make this work easier for today's readers to understand, we developed the **Strategy Playbook**, the Science of Strategy Institute (SOSI) guidebook to explaining Sun Tzu's strategy in the more familiar format of a series of explanations with examples. These lessons are framed in the context of modern competition rather than ancient military warfare.

This Playbook is the culmination of over a decade of work breaking down Sun Tzu's principles into a series of step-by-step practical articles by the Institute's multiple award-winning author and founder, Gary Gagliardi. The original **Art of War** was written for military generals who understood the philosophical concepts of ancient China, which in itself is a practical hurdle that most modern readers cannot clear. Our Art of War Playbook is written for today's reader. It puts Sun Tzu's ideas into everyday, practical language.

The Playbook defines a new science of strategic competition aimed at today's challenges. This science of competition is designed as the complementary opposite of the management science that is taught in most business schools. This science starts, as Sun Tzu did himself, by defining a better, more complete vocabulary for discussing competitive situations. It connects the timeless ideas of Sun Tzu to today's latest thinking in business, mathematics, and psychology.

The entire Playbook consists of two hundred and thirty articles describing over two-thousand interconnected key methods. These articles are organized into nine different areas of strategic skill from understanding positioning to defending vulnerabilities. All together this makes up over a thousand pages of material.

Playbook Access

The Playbook's most up-to-date version is available as separate articles on our website. Live links make it easy to access the connections between various articles and concepts. If you become a SOSI Member, you can access any Playbook article at any time and access their links.

However, at the request of our customers, we also offer these articles as a series of nine <u>eBooks</u>. Each of the nine sections of the entire Playbook makes up a separate eBook, Playbook Parts One Through Nine. These parts flow logically through the Progress Cycle of listen-aim-move-claim (see illustration). Because of the dynamic nature of the on-line version, these eBooks are not going to be as current as the on-line version. You can see a outline of current Playbook articles here and, generally, the eBook version will contain most of the same material in the same order.

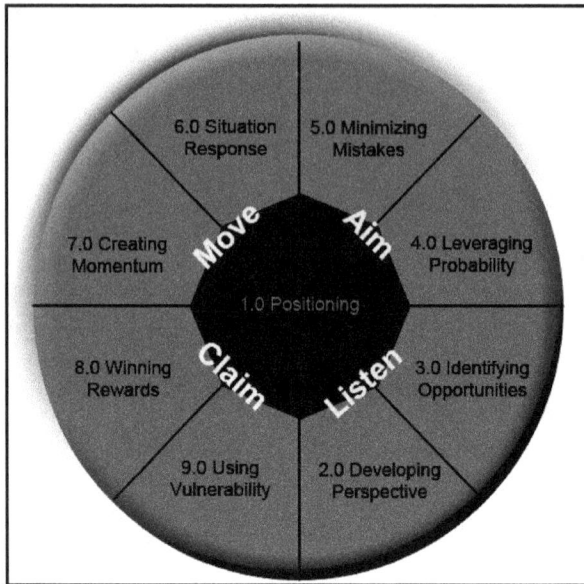

Nine categories of strategic skills define cycle that advances our positions:

1. Comparing Positions,

2. Developing Perspective,

3. Identifying Opportunities,

4. Leveraging Probability,

5. Minimizing Mistakes,

6. Responding To Situations,

7. Creating Momentum,

8. Winning Rewards, And

9. Defending Vulnerabilities.

Playbook Structure and Design

These articles are written in standard format including 1) the general principle, 2) the situation, 3) the opportunity, 4) the list of specific Art of War key methods breaking down the general principle into a series of actions, and 5) an illustration of the application of each of those key methods to a specific competitive situation. Key methods are written generically to apply to every competitive arena (business, personal life, career, sports, relationships, etc.) with each specific illustrations drawn from one of these areas.

A number identifies where each article appears in Playbook Structure. For example, the article 2.1.3 Strategic Deception is the third article in the first section of the second book in the nine volumes of the Strategy Playbook. In our on-line version, these links are live, clicking on them brings you to the article itself. We provide them because the interconnection of concepts is important in learning Sun Tzu's system.

Playbook Training

Training in Sun Tzu's warrior skills does not entail memorizing all these principles. Instead, these concepts are used to develop exercises and tools that allow trainees to put this ideas in practice. While each rule is useful, the heart of Sun Tzu system is the methods that connect all the principles together. Training in these principles is designed to develop a gut instinct for how Sun Tzu's strategy is used in different situations to produce success. Principles are interlinked because they describe a comprehensive conceptual mental model. Warrior Class training puts trainees in a situation where they must constantly make decisions, rewarding them for making decisions consist with winning productively instead of destructively.

About Positions

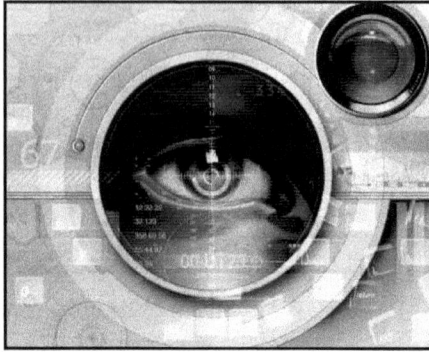

This first volume of Sun Tzu's Playbook focuses on teaching us the nature of strategic positions. "Position awareness" gives you a framework for understanding your strategic situation relative to the conditions around you. It enables you to see your position as part of a larger environment constructed of other positions and the raw elements that create positions. Master Sun Tzu's system of comparing positions, you can understand which aspect of your position are secure and which are the most dynamic and likely to change.

Traditional strategy defines a "position" as a comparison of situations. Game theory defines is as the current decision point that is arrive at as the sum or result of all previous decisions, both yours and those of others. Sun Tzu's methods of positioning awareness are different. They force you to see yourself in the eyes of others. Using these techniques, you broaden your perspective by gathering a range of viewpoints. In a limited sense, the scope of your position defines your area of control within your larger environment. In traditional strategy, five elements--mission, climate, ground, command, and methods--define the dimensions in which competitors can be compared.

Competition as Comparison

Sun Tzu saw that success is based on comparisons. This comparison must take place whenever a choice is made. For Sun Tzu, competition means a comparison of alternative choices or "positions". Battles are won by positioning before they are fought. These positions provide choices for everyone involved. Good positions discourage others from attacking you and invite them to support you. Sun Tzu's system teaches us how to systematically build up our positions to win success in the easiest way possible.

Competing positions are compared on the basis many elements, both objective and subjective. Sun Tzu's strategy is to identify these points of comparison and to understand how to leverage them. Learning Sun Tzu's strategy requires learning the details of how positions are compared and advanced. Sun Tzu taught that fighting to "sort things out" is a foolish way to find learn the strengths and weaknesses of a position. Conflict to tear down opposing positions is the most costly way to win competitive comparisons.

Today's More Competitive World

In the complex, chaotic world of today, we can easily get trapped into destructive rather than productive situations. Even our smallest decisions can have huge impact on our future. The problem is that we are trained for yesterday's world of workers, not today's world of warriors. We are trained in the linear thinking of planning in predictable, hierarchical world. This thinking applies less and less to today's networked, more competitive world.

Following a plan is the worker's skill of working in pre-defined functions in an internal, stable, controlled environment. The competitive strategy of Sun Tzu is the warrior's skill of making good decisions about conditions in complex, fast-changing, competitive environments. Sun Tzu's strategic system teaches us to adapt to the unexpected events that are becoming more and more common in our lives. We live in a world where fewer and fewer key events are planned. Navigating our new world of external challenges requires a different set of skills.

Most of us make our decisions without any understanding of competition. The result is that most of us lose as many battles as we win, never making consistent progress. Events buffet us, turning us in one direction and then the other. Too often, we end up repeating our past patterns of mistakes.

The Science of Strategy Institute teaches you the warrior's skills of adaptive response. There are many organizations that teach planning and organization. The Institute is one of the few places in the world you can get learn competitive thinking, and the only place in the world, with a comprehensive Playbook.

Seeing Situations Differently

Sun Tzu taught that a warrior's decision-making was a matter of reflex. As we develop our strategic decision-making skills, the critical conditions in situations simply "pop" out at us. This isn't magic. The latest research on how decisions are made tells us a lot about why Sun Tzu's principles work. It comes from using patterns to retrain our mind to see conditions differently. The study of successful response arose from military confrontations, where every battle clearly demonstrated how hard it is to predict events in the real world. Sun Tzu saw that winners were always those who knew how to respond appropriately to the dynamic nature of their situation.

Sun Tzu's principles provides a complete model for the key knowledge for understanding conditions in complex dynamic environments. This model "files" each piece of data into the appropriate place in the big picture. As the picture of your situation fills in, you can identify the opportunities hidden within your situation.

Making Decisions about Conditions

Instead of focusing on a series of planned steps, Sun Tzu's principles are about making decisions regarding conditions. It concerns itself with: 1) identifying the relative strengths and weaknesses of competitive positions, 2) advancing positions leveraging opportunities, and 3) the types of responses to specific challenges that work the most frequently. Using Sun Tzu's principles, we call these three areas position awareness , opportunity development , and situation response . Each area that we master broadens your capabilities.

- Position awareness trains us to recognize that competitive situations are defined by the relationship among alternative positions. Developing this perspective never ends. It deepens throughout our lives.
- Opportunity development explores the ground, testing our perceptions. Only testing the edges of perspective through action can we know what is true.
- S ituation response trains us to recognize the key characteristics of the immediate situation and to respond appropriately. Only by practice, can we learn to trust the viewpoint we have developed.

Success in competitive environments comes from making better decisions every day. Sharp strategic reflexes flow from a clear understanding of where and when you use which competitive tools methods.

The Key Viewpoints

As an individual, you have a unique and valuable viewpoint, but every viewpoint is inherently limited by its own position. The result is that people cannot get a useful perspective on their own situations and surrounding opportunities. The first formula of positioning awareness involve learning what information is relevant. The most advanced techniques teach how to gather that information and put it into a bigger picture.

Most people see their current situations as the sum of their past successes and failures. Too often people dwell on their mistakes while simultaneously sitting on their laurels. Sun Tzu's strategy forces you to see your position differently. How you arrived at your current position doesn't matter. Your position is what it is. It is shaped by history but history is not destiny.

In this framework, the only thing that matters is where you are going and how you are going to get there. As you begin to develop your strategic reflexes, you start to think more and more about how to secure your current position and advance it.

Seeing the Big Picture

Most people see all the details of their lives, but they cannot see what those detail mean in terms of the big picture. As you master position awareness, you don't see your life as a point but as a path. You see your position in terms of what is changing and what resources are available. You are more aware of your ability to make decisions and your skills in working with others.

Most importantly, this strategic system forces you to get in touch with your core set of goals and values.

Untrained people usually see their life in terms of absolutes: successes and failures, good luck and bad, weakness and strength. As you begin to master position awareness, you begin to see all comparisons of strength and weakness are temporary and relative. A position is not strong or weak in itself. Its strength or weakness depends on how it compares or "fits" with surrounding positions. Weakness and strength are not what a position is, but how you use it.

The Power of Perspective

Positional awareness gives you the specialized vocabulary you need to understanding how situations develop. Mastering this vocabulary, you begin to see the leverage points connecting past and future. You replace vague conceptions of "strength," "momentum," and "innovation" with much more pragmatic definitions that you can actually use on a day to day basis.

Mastering position awareness also changes your relationships with other people. It teaches you a different way of judging truth and character. This methods allow you to spot self-deception and dishonest in others. It also allows you to understand how you can best work with others to compensate for your different weaknesses.

Once you develop a good perspective of position, it naturally leads you to want to learn more about how you can improve you position through the various aspects of opportunity development covered in the subsequent parts of the Strategy Playbook.

Seeing the Invisible

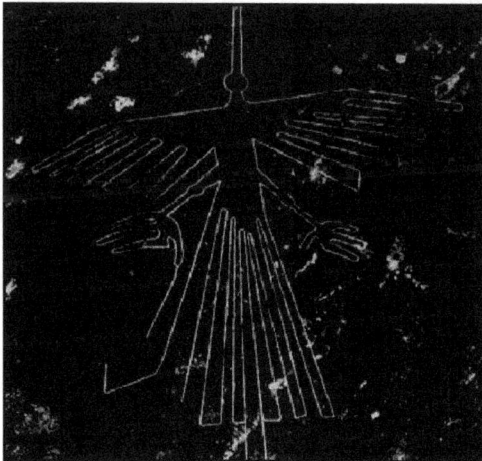

The "Nazca lines" are giant drawings etched across thirty miles of desert on Peru's southern coast. The patterns are only visible at a distance of hundreds of feet in the air. Below that, they look like strange paths or roads to nowhere. Just as we cannot see these lines without the proper perspective, people who master Sun Tzu's methods can suddenly recognize situations that were invisible to them before. Unless we have the right perspective, we cannot compare situations and positions successfully. The most recent scientific research explains why people cannot see these patterns for comparison without developing the network framework of adaptive thinking.[1]

Seeing Patterns

We can imagine patterns in chaotic situations, but seeing real pattern is the difference between success and failure. In our seminars, we demonstrate the power of seeing patterns in a number of exercises.

The mental models used by warrior give them "situation awareness." This situation awareness isn't just vague theory. Recent research shows that it can be measured in a variety of ways.[2] We now know that untrained people fall victim to a flow of confusing information because they don't know where its pieces fit. Those trained in Sun Tzu's mental models plug this stream of information quickly and easily into a bigger picture, transforming the skeleton's provided by Sun Tzu's system into a functioning awareness of your strategic position and its relation to other positions. Each piece of information has a place in that picture. As the information comes in, it fills in the picture, like pieces of a puzzle.

The ability to see the patterns in this bigger picture allows experts in strategy to see what is invisible to most people in a number of ways. They include:

- People trained in Art of War principles--<u>recognition-primed decision-making</u> --see patterns that others do not.
- Trained people can spot anomalies, things that should happen in the network of interactions but don't.
- Trained people are in touch with changes in the environment within appropriate time horizons.
- Trained people recognize complete patterns of interconnected elements under extreme time pressure.

Procedures Make Seeing Difficult

One of the most surprising discoveries from this research is that those who know procedures, that is, a linear view of events, alone have a ***more*** difficult time recognizing patterns than novices. An interesting study[3] examined the different recognition skills of three groups of people 1) experts, 2) novices, and 3) trainers who taught the standard procedures. The three groups were asked to pick out an expert from a group novices in a series of videos showing them performing a decision-making task, in this case, CPR. Experts were able to recognize the expert 90% of the time. Novices recognized the expert 50% of the time. The shocking fact was that trainers performed much worse that the novices, recognizing the expert only 30% of the time.

Why do those who know procedures fail to see what the experts usually see and even novices often see? Because, as research into <u>mental simulations</u> has shown, those with only a procedural model fit everything into that model and ignore elements that don't fit. In the above experiment, interviews with the trainers indicated that they assumed that the experts would always follow the procedural model. In real life, experts adapt to situations where unique conditions often trump procedure. Adapting to the situation rather than following set procedures is a central focus the form of strategy that the Institute teaches.

Missing Expected Elements

People trained to recognize the bigger picture beyond procedures also recognize when expected elements are missing from the picture. These anomalies or, what the cognition experts[4] describe as "negative cues" are invisible to novices *and* to those trained only in procedure. Without sense of the bigger pattern, people are focused too narrowly on the problem at hand. The "dog that didn't bark" from the Sherlock Holmes story, "Silver Blaze," is the most famous example of a negative cue. Only those working from a larger nonprocedural framework can expect certain things to happen and notice when they don't.

The ability to see what is missing also comes from the expectations generated by the mental model. Process-oriented models have the expectation of one step following another, but situation-recognition models create their expectations from signals in the environment. Research[5] into the time horizons of decision-makers shows that different time scales are at work. People at the highest level of organizations must look a year or two down the road, using strategic models that work in that timeframe, doing strategic planning. Decision-makers on the front-lines, however, have to react within minutes or even seconds to changes in their situation, working from their strategic reflexes. The biggest danger is that people get so wrapped up in a process that they lose contact with their environment.

Decisions Under Pressure

Extreme time pressure is what distinguishes front-line decision-making from strategic planners. One of the biggest discoveries in cognitive research[6] is that trained people do much better in seeing their situation instantly and making the correct decisions under time pressure. Researchers found virtually no difference between the decisions that experts made under time pressure when comparing them to decisions made without time pressure. That research also finds that those with less experience and training made dramatically worse decisions when they were put under time pressure.

The central argument for training our strategic reflexes is that our situation results, not from chance or luck, but from the instant decisions that that we all make every day. Our position is the sum of these decisions. If we cannot make the right decisions on the spot, when they are needed, our plans usually come to nothing. This is why we describe training people's strategic reflexes as helping them "do at first what most people only do at last."

The success people experience seeing what is invisible to others is dramatic. To learn more about how the strategic reflexes we teach differ from what can be planned, read about the contrast between planning and reflexes here . As our many members report, the success Sun Tzu's system makes possible is remarkable.

1 Chi, Glaser, & Farr, 1988, The Nature of Expertise, Erlbaum
2 Endsley & Garland, Analysis and Measurement of Situation Awareness
3 Klein & Klein, 1981, "Perceptual/Cognitive Analysis of proficient CPR Performance", Midwestern Psychological Association Meeting, Chicago.
4 Dr. David Noble, Evidence Based Research, Inc.In Gary Klein, Sources of Power, 1999
5 Jacobs & Jaques, 1991, "Executive Leadership".In Gal & Mangelsdofs (eds.), Handbook of Military Psychology, Wiley
6 Calder, Klein, Crandall,1988, "Time Pressure, Skill, and Move Quality in Chess". American Journal of Psychology, 101:481-493

About Probability

You cannot pursue every opportunity you discover. You must be selective. Opportunities represent potential positions. Each position has its own unique character. Each has its own limitations. Each offers its own unique probabilities for success. This chapter covers how you can identify the "high-probability" opportunities for success.

To calculate these probabilities, you must understand your current position's potential as a stepping-stone to future positions. You must evaluate the potential and limitations hidden in every competitive position. You cannot invest in positions that are difficult to defend. You cannot move into positions that are dead ends.

Different Forms of Opportunity

In evaluating the potential of a given opportunity, we start with the concept of "ground form." In Sun Tzu's system, the ground is the basis of competition. Different competitive arenas are different types of ground, but these different types of ground all have a form. Sun Tzu's principles define four forms, each of which offers its own advantages and challenges in terms of choosing an opportunity.

In this volume, we describe these four forms very generally as "tilted," "fluid", "soft," and "neutral." However, in writing about Sun Tzu's principles, we have used a variety of other terms as well, including "uneven," "rapidly changing," "uncertain", and "solid." The terms used are less important than the key methods describing them, but here we provide a quick overview

"Tilted" or "uneven" forms represent an unbalanced areas. Physically, Sun Tzu described them as "mountains." In a modern social context, we have describe them as a business market have many small potential customers are dominated by a few very large customers. These forms are important because the force of gravity give some positions an advantage. We use their gravity to fight "downhill."

"Fluid" or "rapidly changing" areas are dominated by climate, that is, the forces of change. Sun Tzu describes this as water. In modern terms, we talk about areas such as technology that change rapidly. The advantage in these areas comes from the direction of change. We call this direction the "flow" or "currents" of change.

"Soft" of "uncertain" areas are dominated by confusion, rumors, and a lack of solid information. Sun Tzu described them physically as "marshes." In modern society, they are any area where most people have proven to be undependable. The advantage in these areas comes from whatever stability or solid information we can find.

"Neutral" or "solid" areas are the opposite of the other three. They are just right. They are even, stable, and certain. In these area, there is no forces at work, such a gravity, currents, or stability, that give an advantage to one position over another.

You can use the topography of an opportunity against your competitors in any of these four areas. You must not treat all spaces as if they were the same. You must adapt to the unique conditions in the place, just as you adapt to the changing character of your enterprise.

Physical and Psychological Space

Most of the principles in this volume deal with the idea of "space" or "area." In picking an opportunity, you must be able to defend your existing position long enough to move to another one. How easily you can defend your position and eventually move to a better position is determined by the aspects of its "space," discussed in this chapter. Some positions are easy to defend; others are more difficult. Some positions are difficult to advance while others make advancing easy.

There is nothing new in any of these situations. They have occurred a million times in competition, but every situation will not occur in every campaign. You cannot predict if or when they will occur.

Positions exist both in physical space and mind space. Your job has a physical location. Its location describes its physical relationships with customers, competitors, and suppliers. Your role also has a psychological location. Its psychological position maps how your customers, competitors, and suppliers position you in their mental image of the marketplace.

As we move deeper into the information age, physical market space is becoming less important while psychological or mental space is becoming more important. Affinity trumps proximity. Advances in transportation and communication make physical proximity less important.

All positions have shape. Physical spaces have shape. Psychological spaces have shape. Positions, a combination of both, have shape. Though it is easier to discuss shape in physical terms, the most important forces shaping markets today are psychological. Your success depends more upon people's perceptions than upon physical location. It doesn't matter how physically close people are if you are psychologically remote.

Because it exists primarily in people's minds, a position is subjective. Each customer and competitor defines it a little differently. Your position is both subjective and relative. It is defined only by how people mentally compare you with your competitors.

Like physical space, the psychological space of the market also has three dimensions. These dimensions are area, obstacles, and dangers. These terms have very specific meanings in the science of strategy.

"Area" measures the range of psychological territory that a position covers. For example, a position may address a small number of needs for a small group of people. Such a position covers a very small market area. A position may also address a wide variety of needs for a large group of people. Then the position covers a market area. The more area in a position's space, the more difficult that space is to defend.

"Barriers" refer to the number of problems you encounter in moving from one position space to another. Think of these problems or obstacles as "barriers to entry." The more barriers in a space, the more time, effort, or resources it takes to navigate that space. A position space that is easy to get into has few barriers to entry. A position space that is difficult to get into has many barriers to entry. The more barriers in a space, the easier it is to defend but the harder it is to advance into it.

"Dangers" refers to the type of risks you encounter as you move out of certain types of positions. Some positions are challenging because you cannot leave them without weakening your position. Other positions are dangerous because if you attempt to leave them, you destroy them and cannot return to them. Both dangers make advances difficult.

Positions in Six Extremes

There are no absolutes in strategy. Everything is relative. Comparing every unique aspect of your position to all the unique aspects of your competitors is too complicated so we simplify. You can gauge the potential of a given competitive position by comparing it to the six extreme variations of the three dimension. We call these extremes the six benchmarks.

You examine positions one dimension at a time. For area, you compare your position to the smallest position area and largest position area. For barriers, you compare your positions to positions with the most barriers and the fewest. For dangers, you compare positions to the challenges of niches and peaks. By examining each of these six benchmark regions one at a time, you get a sense of the restrictions of any given position.

In this volume, you will learn to Sun Tzu's terminology for comparing positions using these benchmarks. You will also learn their related strengths and weaknesses. This is done in the terms of complementary opposites. Confined positions are the opposite of spread-out positions. Barricaded positions are the opposite of wide-open positions. Fragile positions or niches are the opposite of optimal positions or peaks.

You can see the restrictions in your own position by comparing it to each of these six benchmark regions. A position cannot be, at the same time, both confined and spread out since these are both opposite extremes of area. However, a position or potential position can be confined and barricaded and fragile.

Once you understand the shape of your position or potential position in terms of the six benchmark regions, this analysis will tell you how easily that position will be to establish, defend, and advance. You will also know how you must utilize that particular type of space.

Internal Imbalances

To understand your choices, you have to consider the restrictions created by the nature of any organization upon which you rely. Certain restrictions expose certain weaknesses in an organization. The six flaws of organizations are amplified by the restrictions in the six benchmark position. You can diagnose these weaknesses to predict how a given organization will respond to the restrictions of a position space.

Six weaknesses can handicap any organization. They affect both your own organizations and your competitors' organizations. The presence of these flaws makes it difficult for any organization to take advantage of any position space. However, each of the benchmark handicaps is exaggerated by one particular set of restrictions.

Self-destructive organizations result from a lack of mission. Their problems are most apparent in confined positions. Overextended organizations have to pull back from their position. Their greatest weakness is spread-out positions. Distracted organizations suffer from self-satisfied leadership. They have the most problems in barricaded positions. Barricaded positions are easy to defend but they require concentration. Inefficient organizations waste their resources. They have the most difficulty in wide-open positions. Wide-open positions invite competition. Prices are pressured in markets with few barriers to entry. Undisciplined organizations require not only good leadership judgment, but leadership control over the organization. They are most vulnerable in fragile positions. Fragile market positions require discipline. Untrained organizations have poor systems. They have the most problems in optimal positions. Optimal market positions require minimal decision-making on the part of the enterprise's leadership.

The potential of a given position arises as an interaction between the form of its space and the weaknesses of the organization. An organization can be understood in terms of the relative strength of it leadership, its systems, and the focus and unity it gets from its mission. If you analyze your organizations and your competitors' organizations, you are able to predict their options for defending or advancing their positions.

Knowing a Position's Potential Before Moving

You must understand the potential of your position before moving into a new position. You must understand how to use area, barriers, and dangers in order to advance your current position. You don't want to move into positions that make future advances more difficult. Each position must be a stepping-stone. This is the only way to build success over time.

You must choose or shape the organizations upon which you rely to fit the nature of your position. You do not have to do everything well in every position. You develop the qualities that are critical in your specific position space. You focus on bringing your resources together in confined spaces, on courageous leadership in spread-out positions, on focus in barricaded positions, on efficient systems in wide-open positions, on disciplined leadership in fragile positions, and on effective systems in peak positions. This is how you are profitable in these various situations.

You must respond to the mistakes your competitors make. You challenge them directly when they misjudge their position. Forget your original plans in the given situation. You cannot plan for every opportunity. You must go after opportunities that arise from a competitor's mistakes.

If you examine your current position and potential position, you can know when pursuing a new position will be too costly. Spread-out positions look big enough for unlimited expansion, but they result in a mismatch of your resources with position size. Open positions look easy to get into, but you have to have efficient systems to survive in them. You have to have the resources to invest to surmount the barriers to entry in barricaded positions. You must avoid pursuing positions hat will cost you more than they will ever return.

Your advances must pay for themselves in terms of giving you more resources not just win recognition. Get out of any positions that cannot pay off. Success demands that you make create an advantage, adding value to your environment. This is how you build your position over time. This is how you ensure your success.

All positions have shape and form. The shape of the positions you inhabit determines how easy it will be to defend and expand your position.

There are proven benchmarks for gauging position potential. Six benchmark positions represent the purest forms of extreme, static conditions. These benchmarks define the ways in which each of these six positions must be utilized.

Every organization has weaknesses and strengths. To make the most of the potential hidden within your position, you must know what elements within your organization need to be developed.

Your ability to harvest position's potential determines your future. You may know that the organizations to which you belong really work within a given type of space. You must also know that your competitors are poorly suited for that space. Finally, you must also know exactly how to use your resources in that space. If you understand your position and its dynamics, your success is assured.

4.0 Leveraging Probability

Sun Tzu's nine principles for making better decisions regarding our choice of opportunities.

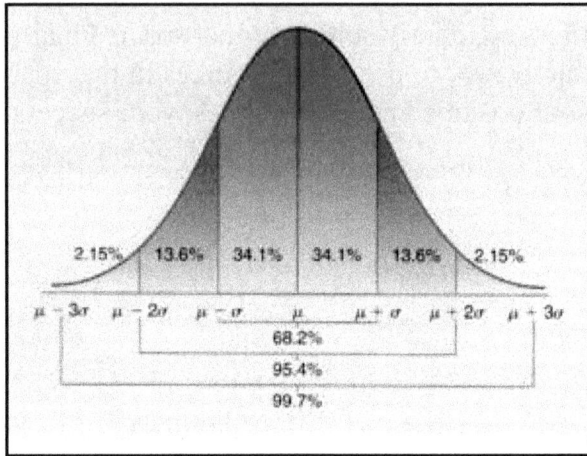

"Your numbers determine your calculations.
Your calculations determine your decisions.
Your decisions determine your victory."
Sun Tzu's The Art of War 4:4:12-14

"Probability is expectation founded upon partial knowledge."
George Boole

General Rule: We must choose the least expensive opportunities that lead to the most rewarding positions.

Situation:

An opportunity is any opening that we have the resources to pursue, but it is a mistake to pursue every possible opportunity. Most openings are unlikely to offer real rewards. Sun Tzu's science is exploration, designed to increase our probability of success over time. We cannot be successful if we chase after every opening, going in one direction then in another. Our resources are limited. We can only do one thing at a time. Openings must lead to positions. We cannot afford to pursue positions that we are not likely to win. We also must not choose positions that are not likely to take us where we want to go.

Opportunity:

The key is identifying high-probability opportunities. These are opportunities that lead to positions that pay for themselves. This is the topic of all of the articles in this section of our Playbook. We have limited time and resources (3.1.1 Resource Limitations). We want to devote those resources to pursuing opportunities. Those opportunities must lead to positions that we can win. Those positions must be those that are the most likely to pay, both in the short term and long term (3.1.2 Strategic Profitability). While nothing can tell us the true potential of an opportunity before we explore it, we can compare opportunities by characteristics that have, in the past, proven to make a big difference in identifying those opportunities that lead to great positions.

Key Methods:

These ten key methods define how we leverage probability to our advantage.

1. ***To leverage probability, we must think both of opportunities and positions as stepping stones.*** Opportunities are openings to a position. Positions move us toward our goals. We must consider where each step leads before we take it. Pursuing any opportunities has costs. Only positions can return rewards. Using high probability opportunities determines how easily and inexpensively new, valuable positions are won, defended, and advanced (1.1 Position Paths).

2. ***To leverage probability, we need only the ability to compare the general odds.*** Success doesn't require that we make perfect choices about our moves, but choosing the probabilities makes our

success more certain over time. We can never know exactly where a specific opportunity will lead so we compare opportunities based upon how we see the probabilities involved. Only from these comparisons can we get a quick idea of the future potential profitability of exploring an opportunity (1.3.1 Competitive Comparison).

3. ***Our probability of a successful move depends both on our starting point and destination.*** Successful moves improve our position. Our current position only makes certain opportunities available. Our choices in pursuing opportunities can either open or close doors for us. Both our current position and desired future position have different limitations that we must consider in making our moves. We want to move in directions that open us to more and better opportunities over time. (4.1 Limitations and Potential).

4. ***To leverage probability, we must choose non-action when high-probability opportunities are unavailable.*** Though we talk in terms of choosing among opportunities, we always have the opportunity to choose not to pursue any current opening. When we choose non-action, we are conserving resources so we have them to pursue future opportunities (4.2 Choosing Non-Action).

5. ***To leverage probability, we must work with rather than against the forces in our environment.*** We increase our chances of success if we leverage the forces in our current position and future positions. We must consider how these forces can work for or against us before we make our move (4.3 Ground Forms).

6. ***To leverage probability, we must choose close opportunities instead of distant ones.*** Proximity is one of the primary keys in determining probability. How close we are to openings, both physically and psychologically, largely determines whether or not we are likely to succeed using a given opportunity to move forward. The closer a future opportunity is to our current position, the easier it is to win. Proximity is measured both in physical space and mental knowledge. In moving forward, we must as much as possible stick to what we know and understand (4.4 Strategic Distance).

7. ***To leverage probability, we must judge opportunities based upon their appearances.*** We cannot know opportunities before we explore them but we can see certain surface conditions. Before we

explore a position, we must consider its size, its barriers to entry, and how "sticky" it is. Size must match capability. Barriers of entry can be expensive to surmount, but they can also provide protection once they are surmounted. "Stickiness" is more complicated to judge, but it determines how easy it will be to move forward from a position (4.5 Opportunity Surfaces).

8. *To leverage probability, we must consider our internal weaknesses before moving to a new position.* Internal weaknesses are weaknesses of command and methods. No judgments about future position can be made without also considering the capabilities of the person or organization seeking to fill that position. The characteristics of organizations and their leaders make them better suited for some positions than others (4.7 Competitive Weaknesses).

9. *To leverage probability, we must consider the long-term trends in selecting opportunities.* Some directions are supported by long-term climate changes, others are not. We choose to pursue opportunities based not only upon their immediate rewards, but upon their future potential. Ideally, we want to move in directions that open us to more and better opportunities over time. Opportunities that we are likely to have pay off, both in the short term and long term (4.8 Climate Support).

Illustration:

Let us illustrate these principles by thinking about the challenges faced by salespeople in picking which prospects to pursue.

10. *To leverage probability, we must think both of opportunities and positions as stepping stones.* We pursue the prospects that we are most likely to close and which lead us to move prospects and better prospects in the future.

11. *To leverage probability, we need only the ability to compare the general odds.* As a salesperson, we cannot expect every prospect to buy, but we want to pursue only the prospects that are the most likely to buy. We can only know the most general characteristics about prospects before pursuing them so we have to compare them generally or as general groups to decide how to act.

12. ***Our probability of a successful move depends both on our starting point and destination.*** Our most probable future customers are determined by who our current customers are. Our choice of the prospects we pursue determines both the size and quality of the customer base we work ourselves into. For example, if a car salesperson has sold some expensive luxury cars in the past, he can increase his focus on those customers in the future.

13. ***To leverage probability, we must choose non-action when high-probability opportunities are unavailable.*** A salesperson cannot afford to choose every customer. Every low-probability, low-profit customer he wastes time on means less time for pursuing high-probability, high-profit customers.

14. ***To leverage probability, we must work with rather than against the forces in our environment.*** If we go after customers who have high-turnover, we must work against the environment.

15. ***To leverage probability, we must choose close opportunities instead of distant ones.*** We need to go after customers who are both physically and psychologically close to us. ***To leverage probability, we must judge opportunities based upon their appearances.*** A salesperson must consider the size of the prospect base, its ability to pay, and how likely it is to produce repeat customers.

16. ***To leverage probability, we must consider our internal weaknesses before moving to a new position.*** A salesperson cannot pursue prospects who don't fit with either his temperament or his company's processes.

17. ***To leverage probability, we must consider the long-term trends in selecting opportunities.*** A salesperson should sell to customers and markets that are growing rather than shrinking.

4.1 Future Potential

Five key methods regarding the limitations and potential of current and future positions.

"Some commanders are not skilled in making
adjustments to find an advantage.
They can know the shape of the terrain.
Still, they cannot exploit the opportunities of their
ground."

Sun Tzu's The Art of War 8:1:16-18

"Continuous effort - not strength or intelligence - is the
key to unlocking our potential."

Winston Churchill

General Rule: Current and future positions have different limitations that potentially determine future moves.

Situation:

Making choices means eliminating existing options in the hope of discovering better future options. Our past decisions have restricted our current options. Our current decisions will restrict our future options. Every move to a new position puts us on a new path. If we get on the wrong path, we can find fewer and fewer opportunities in the future. We cannot pretend that we can always go back and correct our mistakes.

Opportunity:

Every move to a new position can open up new opportunities while closing down others. Most moves do both. Our first consideration must be where pursuing an opportunity leads in terms of future opportunities. Even successful positions are temporary (1.1.1 Position Dynamics). We must evaluate our opportunity based both upon the potential rewards they offer and the future opportunities they offer. The path has many branches. Each time we choose among different opportunities, we are choosing a certain future. Our opportunity is in thinking before we move about the best way to choose not only among future positions but future paths (1.1 Position Paths).

Key Methods:

The following six key methods describe Sun Tzu's view of future potential.

1. We choose based on probabilities because our knowledge of potential is limited. In improving our choices, choosing the best path is a matter of working from what we know for certain to what is the most uncertain. We move in the general direction of "improving our position" as determined by the general goals of our mission rather than to a specific position because the value of positions is always unknown (2.1.1 Information Limits).

2. All progress begins with the potential of our current position. We do not know where our journey will end, but we know for certain where it must begin. Our current position consists of two components that are critical in picking the best possible opportunities (1.0 Strategic Positioning).

3. We must understand all of the potential in our current position. We can know our current position better than we know where an opportunity will lead. Our *potential* includes all elements of our current position, including both resources and abilities, that facilitate movement. Our *limitations* are the elements of our current position that hinders our movement (3.1.1 Resource Limitations).

4. We must choose openings in the direction that maximize current potential. The potential and limitations of our current position depend on our direction. A seeming limitation can become an advantage given a certain choice of direction. Our limitations make it easier for us to make decisions because they eliminate choices with a low probability of success. We are often too close to our situation in time to see how conditions naturally reverse themselves in different directions. If we are able to overcome what appears to be a limitation related to our current positions today, it can be transformed into more potential in the future (3.2.5 Dynamic Reversal).

5. We must choose opportunities that do not constrict our future potential. Long campaigns especially should open up more potential opportunities since they are a long-term commitment to a direction. We should avoid commitments to directions that offer only one possible goal, which may prove, as we get closer to it, less attractive than it seemed at a distance. The problem with choosing these types of paths is that, by investing heavily in meeting a certain set of requirements, we can get "locked into" a path. The more we invest in a certain path, the more difficult it becomes to leave that path. In the end, such a path may offer relatively few rewards given the costs (6.2 Campaigns).

6. We must choose openings that lead to more and better potential choices. The most common paths to success are not commitments to long campaigns that follow sets of required steps. This often means choosing directions whose requirements we can meet along the way rather than in advance. The best opportunities are short moves in directions where even more openings seem to lie.

Each of these moves should have the potential to be profitable in its own right. Even if they are not immediately profitable, they explore a profitable direction, offering more potential directions of movement (5.4 Minimizing Action).

Illustration:

Let us look at these key methods and how they might apply to the path of someone who has the potential to become President of the U.S. t

1. We choose based on probabilities because our knowledge of potential is limited. No one can plan a path from childhood to the presidency, but we can make choices that maximize our potential in that direction.

2. All progress begins with the potential of our current position. We cannot control our circumstances at birth, but as long as we are not born a foreign citizen, any current position qualifies for being President.

3. We must understand all of the potential in our current position. If we were born into a rich, politically connected family, we have more potential. If we went to Idaho University instead of Yale or Harvard, we have less potential. Coming from a broken home used to be an obstacle, but it no longer is.

4. We must choose openings in the direction that maximize current potential. Going to Harvard and/or Yale and getting a degree in law opens up more opportunities in general but not everyone has those options. Certain disadvantages, such as having a physical handicap, being from a broken home, or being born a minority may have once seemed like limitations to becoming president, but they are no longer. Some day, perhaps even graduating from Idaho University may cease being an obstacle.

5. We must choose opportunities that do not constrict our future potential. While we may not be able to go to Harvard, we can all avoid dropping out of school. Choosing certain types of behavior and getting caught at it publicly can eliminate future opportunities.

6. *We must choose openings that lead to more and better potential choices.* Most law or business degrees from an Ivy League college don't lead to the White House, but they lead to a lot of other good things as well.

4.2 Choosing Non-Action

Sun Tzu's seven key methods about choosing between action and non-action.

"There are roads that you must not take.
There are armies that you must not fight.
There are strongholds that you must not attack.
There are positions that you must not defend.
There are government commands that must not be obeyed."

Sun Tzu's The Art of War 8:1:9-14

"Insanity: doing the same thing over and over again and expecting different results. "

Albert Einstein

General Principle: To pursue opportunities, we must choose when and when not to act.

Situation:

We must walk the line between drifting along in life and fighting useless battles. Though we may not realize it, most of the decisions that we make are choices of non-action. In many situations, choosing not to react can be the best choice. However, the habits and inertia of non-action can become deadly. It is always easier to continue doing what we have done in the past than go in a different direction. We must not act only when action is forced upon us because those situations are defined by our lack of options. We must make the choice to pursue opportunities. If is too easy to fail to act in the face of opportunity because our bias is toward non-action omission bias. These choices require a change of direction, which is hard. However, chasing after every possible opportunity doesn't lead to success either because we have limited resources and time. Danger lies in both directions.

Opportunity:

We dramatically improve success by knowing how to balance action and non-action. We must decide which opportunities to pursue and which not to pursue. when we are not pursuing a new direction, we must gather information about new directions to pursue. Learning to see opportunities is half the challenge (3.0 Identifying Opportunities). Eventually, we must pursue the best opportunity that we have long before taking action is forced upon us by our situation. We must know instantly what situations to avoid. We must know quickly which opportunities to pursue. We must change our direction by choice not circumstance.

Key Methods:

Before we can understand the more detailed methods for separating high-probability opportunities from their lower-probability cousins, we first must understand the principles governing action and non-action and our choices.

1. Non-action frees up the resources that we need for future action. We must see non-action and actions as requiring each other. Our decisions to act are made possible by earlier decisions not to act. Actions use resources. Constant action is prevented by limitations of resources. When we choose non-action, it makes most resources available for future actions (3.1.1 Resource Limitations).

2. Most of our decisions for non action are based on habit and reflex. Most of our decisions are made automatically without analysis.We simply act out of habit and training without having to think about it. This isn't a bad thing. Instant gut decisions are better decisions, especially in areas that require expertise (6.1.1 Conditioned Reflexes).

3. Too many decisions for non-action simply continue or repeat past behavior unthinkingly. On a second-to-second or minute-to-minute level, we need to continue what we are doing to get tasks done. On this micro-decision level, finishing what we are doing at the moment is important. We would never complete any task if we are continually distracted by events. In larger blocks of time, we must get from one task to the next. On this macro-decisions level, our habits are less beneficial. We can fall into set patterns of behavior that lock us into doing what we have always done, which can only get us what we have always gotten or less because of the laws of diminishing returns (2.3.3 Likely Reactions).

4. We must choose non-action because most events do not require a response. Because modern communications expose us to more events, we must be more selective in our reactions. Most events are simply noise, the back and forth lapping of the waves. We must reserve our actions for the important shifts in conditions, the rising and falling of the tides. Another way of saying this is that we must do what is important not merely what is urgent. We must resist two psychological biases, the primacy effect and recency effect , which unduly influences our choices of actions. The primacy effect is our tendency to respond to the first demands on our time. The recency effect is our tendency to respond to the more recent demands on our time (5.1.1 Event Pressure).

5. We must use non-action to create time to weigh potential opportunities. Instead of using all our time in habit or responding to events, we must set aside time to weigh new opportunities. We need to develop a habit of thinking about opportunities. Opportunities seldom interrupt our lives as events do. By their very nature, they are hidden. We must take the time to think about them and consciously decide whether or not they are worth pursuing (3.2.2 Opportunity Invisibility).

6. We must consciously reject low-probability opportunities, choosing non-action. We must not make the mistake of thinking that we must pursue every opportunity that comes along. We can do only one-thing at time. We have limited resources. Most opportunities have a low-probability of success. If we commit ourselves to pursue a low-value opportunity, we will not have the resources to pursue a better opportunity when it comes along. We must know which opportunities we can eliminate from consideration (3.1.1 Resource Limitations).

7. We must stop doing other tasks to make time to act on an opportunity that has a high probability of success. We must make time because we cannot take time to act quickly on high probability opportunities. If we want to advance our position, we ***must*** pursue opportunities. This requires the time to do so. However, we must not act on every opportunity. We must pursue ***only*** those opportunities that meet the criteria defining high-probability opportunities. We cannot know how long an opportunity will last. All opportunities have a limited shelf life. We do not know when a better opportunity will come along. We must explore all high-probability opportunities as quickly as we can. They will not improve over time (3.1.6 Time Limitations).

Illustration:

Let me illustrate these principles in the context of what I am doing now, re-writing this Playbook article.

1. *Non-action frees up the resources that we need for future action.* I had to choose not to do something else in order to write this article.

2. *Most of our decisions for non action are based on habit and reflex.* My decision to re-write these articles was already made months ago when I committed to our Today's Article on Warrior's Rules program. When I am not traveling, I know when I get up that I am going to do at least one such article and schedule it for publication.

3. *Too many decisions for non-action simply continue or repeat past behavior unthinkingly. My day often starts on auto-pilot.* Normally, I get up around six, review the morning's news on-line, and often start editing an article. Since these are rewrites, I spend my first minutes rearranging the existing text to our new standards without thinking much about content. Most mornings I am interrupted by a few phone calls, perhaps a radio interview. A couple of hours after being up, I start coffee and maybe do some kitchen cleanup. Until this point, I am still waking up, operating largely out of habit. Then I start to deal with the day's events and look for opportunities.

4. *We must choose non-action because most events do not require a response.* As I review the morning news, often in the context of preparing for the coming day, I am looking for opportunities to do an "Strategy in the News" article. In the past, before I was as busy as I am today, I felt pressure to write a new news article every day as well. Now, I choose not to because I have better uses for the time.

5. *We must use non-action to create time to weigh potential opportunities.* If I don't see any opportunities to dramatically improve a Rules article, I simply correct a few things or add an image. This allows me to get onto other routine work, such as answering my email or testing new website features, as quickly as possible. Today, I found this article extremely incomplete, not mentioning several key points on non-action and offering no illustration of the principles.

6. We must consciously reject low-probability opportunities, choosing non-action. The <u>format for Playbook articles</u> makes openings for improvement rather clear. Many existing articles are missing components: descriptions of the situation and opportunity, poorly explained steps or missing illustrations of the steps. All are quick, easy openings to fill. In filling them, these articles are generating a bigger and bigger following for Sun Tzu's ideas.

7. We must stop doing other tasks to make time to act on an opportunity that has a high probability of success. If I find an opportunity for a "Strategy in the News" article, I always do it immediately rather than try to get back to it. Same with adding to a daily Rules article. If I see a way to improve it, I do it now, knowing that I won't get back to it for some months and by then will have lost the idea.

4.3 Leveraging Form

Sun Tzu's seven key methods on how we can leverage the form of a territory.

"You can find an advantage in all four of these situations."

Sun Tzu's The Art of War 9:1:25

"Let us, my friends, snatch our opportunity from the passing day."

Horace

General Principle: We should favor opportunities that leverage gravity, the currents of change, and exclusive dependability.

Situation:

The most important form of space only exists in our minds. Strategy leverages our mental mapping of the contested territory. We must evaluate opportunities based on the form of our opportunity. The forms of physical strategic space is easier to understand, but they are becoming less important in our competitive decisions. The forms of psychological strategic space are more difficult to understand, but they are becoming increasingly important. As we move deeper into the information age, understanding the shape of our opportunities in psychological space is difficult without useful analogies that connect to our sense of physical space.

Opportunity:

In applying Sun Tzu's ideas, we use physical analogies to represent many aspects of psychological spaces. These analogs use both the objective and subjective dimensions to compare the characteristics of potential positions (1.2 Subobjective Positions). We can see and more easily comprehend relationships in physical space. We use this understanding to apprehend the key difficulties with our opportunities that exist primarily in the psychological space of competition. In using these analogies to pick the best opportunities, it is often easier to use the process of elimination. We look for defects in opportunities that eliminate them from consideration. No opportunity is perfect, but some opportunities are too difficult to pursue.

Key Methods:

This following eight key methods describe what we must know to leverage the form of an opportunity.

1. Our opportunity for leverage depends on the form of the contested territory. An opportunity is an opening. Though its space is empty, its forms exists in the context of a given type of territory. How we can leverage the territory to take advantage of an opportunity depends on that form. Form is important both in choosing opportunities and in choosing our actions to react to situations (6.7.1 Forms Adjustments).

2. The opportunity to leverage form exists as inequality in a territory. This inequality can be seen as a type of openings, from which all opportunities spring. Sun Tzu describes four forms of territory: mountains, rivers, marshes, and plateaus. In physical space, these forms of territory determine how easily we can move into a new position, defend it, and move on from it. We adapt these same concepts from physical space into the psychological space of competition. The first three of these four forms are dominated by features which can be leveraged. In each of these three spaces, one direction or specific location has a specific advantage over other locations in their immediate vicinity. We abstract these physical forms into mental models that we can apply to analogous situations in psychological space (2.2.2 Mental Models).

3. *Tilted forms define territories in which we can leverage gravity.* These spaces are dominated by uneven features that Sun Tzu describes as mountains. In physical terms, the force of gravity gives an advantage in these areas to some positions over others. In psychological terms, gravity exists were opinions tilt strongly in one direction. These are often areas where the opinions of a few key people or organizations are much more important than those of most people or organizations (4.3.1 Tilted Forms).

4. *Fluid forms define territories in which we can leverage the direction of flow.* These spaces are dominated by the flow of change that Sun Tzu describes as rivers. In physical terms, the direction of the flow gives an advantage to one position over another. In psychological terms, currents exists wherever the direction of change favors some positions over others (4.3.2 Fluid Forms).

5. *Soft forms define territories in which we can leverage the rare areas of support.* Soft forms are dominated by non-supporting features. In physical terms, dependable ground is rare in these areas and therefore valuable. In psychological terms, dependability is important because most features in the environment is uncertain and easily changed (4.3.3 Soft Forms).

6. *Neutral forms define territories that offer few opportunities for leverage.* On neutral ground, the three characteristics that can be leveraged to create an advantage--gravity, current, and dependability--are unimportant. They can exist in small degrees, but the advantage or disadvantage that they offer is not necessarily decisive. One neutral ground, success is determined by characteristics other than form. We cannot leverage form against others, and they cannot leverage form against us (4.3.4 Neutral Form).

7. High probability opportunities are those where we can leverage form against our opponents. In non-neutral forms, the best opportunities are those favored by gravity, current direction, or exclusive dependability. The worst opportunities are those in which these forces can be leveraged against us. We compare opportunities and potential positions based upon these characteristics (1.3.1 Competitive Comparison).

Illustration:

Let us illustrate these ideas by using them to describe different types of markets.

1. Our opportunity for one type of leverage depends on the form of the contested territory. All marketplaces have a shape in which we can look for opportunities.

2. The opportunity to leverage form exists as inequality in a territory. To see the form of a marketplace, we must think about why one position in that market is better than another.

3. Tilted forms define territories in which we can leverage gravity. The U.S. market for textbooks is an tilted form of ground. While each state makes its own public school purchasing decisions, a few large states, specifically California, Texas, and Florida, set the standards for all the rest because of the size of their markets.

4. Fluid forms define territories in which we can leverage the direction of flow. The high-tech market is a fluid form of ground. They typical high-tech company must reinvent their product line every three years, making decisions about the direction of the fast-changing current of tastes and technology.

5. Soft forms define territories in which we can leverage the rare areas of support. The political arena is an soft form of ground. Political promises are not more solid than the predictions about the effect of various laws and programs. Voters are best sticking to the few areas of certainty, if they can find them.

6. Neutral forms define territories that offer few opportunities for leverage. A grocery store is a neutral form of ground. It is dominated by the average decision-maker, relatively slow changing products, and a high-level of consistency.

7. *High probability opportunities are those where we can leverage form against our opponents*. Textbook makers need the favor of the big states to generate an economic volume of sales. Tech companies need the support of the trends. Voters want something to depend on. Decision is easy. Don't print the unfavored books. Don't promote the old technology. Don't vote to the fuzziest promise.

4.3.1 Tilted Forms

Sun Tzu's six key methods regarding space that is dominated by uneven features.

"To win your battles, never attack uphill."
Sun Tzu's Art of War 9:1:4

"The object in life is not to be on the side of the majority, but to escape finding oneself in the ranks of the insane."
Marcus Aurelius

General Principle: Seize the high ground.

Situation:

If we can see where the ground is tilted heavily in favor of some positions, we can more easily spot high probability opportunities. In physical space, this tilt of ground is as easy to see because it creates slopes, hills, and mountains. It is harder to determine in the psychological dimension of competition where the ground is tilted based on opinion. In some areas, we have as many different opinions as people. In others, opinions tend to pile up into different camps. Sometimes the resulting tilt of the ground is based simply on the number of people with a set opinion. The problem is that our herd instinct is based on the idea that each person's opinion is equal to that of others. On many types of tilted ground, this average opinion matters less than the opinions that dominate among the key decision-makers, those that decide the competition.

Opportunity:

When the ground is tilted, we must get the force of gravity on our side. Even those with only the most basic understanding of strategy see the value of working from the high ground. When we control the physical high-ground, the force of gravity works in our favor. The same is true of psychological space, only the tilt is determined by opinion, specifically the opinions of the decision-makers who "judge" the context.

Sometimes this "tilt" is the opinion of the crowd. Quite often, however, it is the tilt of the opinions of a few key decision makers or influencers. High-probability opportunities can be defined by our ability to seize the high ground in any situation, recognizing the use of gravity in social situations and psychological situations as well as physical ones.

Key Methods:

In the psychological space of modern competition, we have to think about the mental landscape of a territory instead of the physical space.

1. On tilted forms of ground, some positions are "higher" than others. Height exists when one part of an area rises above others. In physical situations, the difference is in physical height. In social situation, "height" is determined by the relative weight of people's opinions. On relatively flat ground, opinions are varied, without any opinions clearly dominating the others. On tilted ground, a few opinions of groups or certain individuals can rise above those of others (1.3.1 Competitive Comparison).

2. When the tilt depends on broadly shared views, gravity takes the form of popular opinion. This is the realm of our herd instinct.Different groups can have different opinions just as there are different mountains within a mountain range. To know the lay of the land, we must know the tilt of the group in which we find ourselves. We must understand its strong prejudices and how they distinguish that group from surrounding groups (1.6.1 Shared Mission).

3. When the tilt comes from key positions, gravity arises from a relatively few individuals. In these situations, a few people's opinions are counted much more heavily than the opinion of the crowd. In these situations, "height" comes from another bias, called *authority bias.* Under the influence of authority bias, the average decision is heavily influenced by few rather than by the many. We call those with gravity "authorities," "the powerful," "experts," "influencers," or "opinion leaders" (1.5.1 Command Leadership).

4. On tilted forms of ground, gravity gives an advantage to the high ground. This works for both senses of "gravity," the physical force and the psychological force where more of seriousness is given to a few opinions, either broadly shared or arising from a few people. This disparity between the perceived value of some opinions over others creates high ground that can be leveraged. This gravity can arise either from the physical power of these positions, say from control or wealth of resources, or from the subjective power of these positions to tilt the influence of others (1.2 Subobjective Positions).

5. On tilted ground, we must position ourselves on the high ground. Seizing the high ground, means taking positions that are supported by the force of gravity. We want to get either the physical force or the social force on our side. To see the In terms of choosing the best tilted opportunities, we must clearly see where the forces of gravity are. If there are obvious centers of gravity, an advantageous opportunity is defined by an opening that is supported by the opinions of one of those centers of gravity. A defective opportunity is defined as one that goes against the gravity of one of those centers of gravity (4.0 Leveraging Probability).

6. On tilted ground, we can find common denominators among competing centers of gravity. In situations where there are competing tilts among major centers of gravity, taking one side or another can be as dangerous as it is advantageous. In general, we want to find the common inclinations that these major players share. In physical terms, we want to stick to the valleys, which represent the common ground among the big players (3.1.3 Conflict Cost).

Illustration:

Many famous battles are fought on hills because the high ground always gives an strong advantage to the force that occupies it first. Gettysburg was one of the most famous that was decided largely on the basis of the fact that the Union was able to occupy the high ground.

But we see this same effect in every competitive arena where height is at work.

1. On tilted forms of ground, some positions are "higher" than others. In business, certain marketplaces have tilted forms when they are dominated by a few dominant tastes. For example, there are a many good ways to make pizza and no single way dominates the market in America as a whole. However, as you travel across the country, you will find strong regional preferences such as Chicago style or New York style.

2. When the tilt depends on broadly shared views, gravity takes the form of popular opinion. Most Americans prefer tomato sauce on their spaghetti. If we want to open an Italian restaurant, we must offer tomato sauce as an option if we want to satisfy customers. No matter how good our Alfredo sauce or clam sauce, most are going to order tomato sauce.

3. When the tilt comes from key positions, gravity arises from a relatively few individuals. In the textbook market in the U.S., certain large states--Texas, California, Florida, and New York--set the standard for the textbook industry. When a publisher wins a book contract in one of those states, they have seized the high ground.

4. On tilted forms of ground, gravity gives an advantage to the high ground. If we work as employees, the management hierarchy of our organization represents a slope of gravity. The opinions of those higher in the hierarchy have more gravity than those lower on the hierarchy.

5. On tilted ground, we must position ourselves on the high ground. Within a large organization, high-probability opportunities are those that favor the goals, opinions, and prejudices of those high-up within the hierarchy. Seizing the high ground, means taking positions that support or side with the organization's force of gravity.

6. On tilted ground, we can find common denominators among competing centers of gravity. One division leader may favor one type of product while a competing division leader will favor another. They will both support a marketing program that promotes their differing priorities equally well.

4.3.2 Fluid Forms

Sun Tzu's six key methods on selecting opportunities in fast-changing environments.

"Never face against the current."
Sun Tzu's The Art of War, 9:1:13

"The art of progress is to preserve order amid change."
Alfred North Whitehead

General Principle: We must leverage the direction of change instead of fighting against it.

Situation:

Accelerating change affects more and more of the world. When we are trying to select the best opportunities, change creates a problem. Decision-making depends on good information. Good information is easier to get in stable environments because information is so quickly outdated in fast-changing situations. However, opportunity also depends on change. Faster-changing situations create more opportunities than stable ones. As change increases past a certain point, good information about the future becomes impossible to get. Environments that create the most opportunities are, by definition, the same ones on which we have the worst information.

Opportunity:

Even though our information about fast-changing situations is relatively poor, in these situations, we actually need less information. Only one factor is important, especially when considering high-probability opportunities. This factor is the direction of change, the direction of the currents of change. In situations dominated by change, a high-probability opportunity is supported by the direction of change. Our judgments can safely focus on that single issue.

Key Methods:

The following six key methods define the ways in which we use opportunities on fluid ground.

1. Fluid ground combines the elements of climate and ground. We normally think of change as an aspect of climate. All competitive arenas are influenced by climate, but fluid forms of ground are much more strongly influenced by climate shifts than any other form of ground. Fluid opportunities are in areas whose dominant feature is the dynamics of change. Any competitive arena where the conditions change quickly, dragging everything with them into the future, defines this form of ground (1.4.1 Climate Shift).

2. On fluid ground, positions are carried forward by the trends of change themselves. In most competitive arenas, we advance our position only by putting energy into making our moves. On fluid ground, the ground itself is moving. We can create superior positions with very little work by using the direction of change to our advantage (1.1.1 Position Dynamics).

3. The more fluid the ground, the more temporary our current position. Change erodes existing positions. On fluid forms of ground, the force of change can erode our position as fast as we build it up. We end up running the Red Queen's race, running faster and faster just to stay in the same place. In a best case scenario, the force of change carries us forward, building up our position for us while we just maintain our position (1.1.1 Position Dynamics).

4. On fluid ground, we must get the currents on our side. On fluid ground, we have to be concerned about the direction of change. We call this direction the flow of the *current*. The direction of the currents favors some directions of change over others (8.7.1 Evaluating Existing Positions).

5. On fluid ground, the question is never where the opportunity is today, but where it will be in the future. On fluid ground, opportunities are created and outdated extremely quickly. We must look further ahead in making our moves, positioning ourselves to take advantage of an opportunity quickly, before it passes us by (1.8.1 Creation and Destruction).

6. During peak periods of change, we must not attempt a move on fluid ground. The currents of change on fluid ground will wax and wane, but when change reaches it height, we should never attempt to pursue a fluid opportunity. In the book, Golden Key to Strategy , these situations are described as *change storms*. Pursuing an opportunity during a change storm is extremely risky with a low-probability of success. Change storms are growing more common as the pace of change is increasing everywhere. (4.2 Choosing Non-Action).

Illustration:

Let us take our illustrations from my background in the world of high-tech software. I got out of the software business in the late nineties because of my understanding that I was working on fluid ground.

1. Fluid ground combines the elements of climate and ground. During the late nineties, the software business was the perfect example of a fluid opportunity. The average lifespan of technology was about three years.

2. On fluid ground, positions are carried forward by the trends of change themselves. To stay current with the fast-changing technology, we had to completely redevelop our software products every three years. We "surfed" the various waves of change in the industry.

3. The more fluid the ground, the more temporary our current position. When we sold our company in 1997, the company that purchased it didn't understand the nature of fast-changing terrain. The result is that they ended up closing down the division that our company represented after three years because they didn't know how to keep the current of change on their side.

4. On fluid ground, we must get the currents on our side. In software right now, the direction of change favors applications that utilize the server cloud of the web rather than those that stand isolated on the desktop. It also favors applications that can be used both on phones as well as desktops. Today's software, and perhaps even today's businesses, are about making connections rather than simply performing tasks.

5. On fluid ground, the question is never where the opportunity is today, but where it will be in the future. On phone, the first dominant platform was the iPhone, but the android rapidly became more popular because it is a broad standard sold by many different vendors. Those developing applications that focus solely on the iPhone could easily miss the shift. The question as of this writing is where Windows 8 will be the future.

6. During peak periods of change, we must not attempt a move on fluid ground. Change storms can take many forms. Personal change storms can arise from death, divorce, a move to a new town, marriage, the birth of a child, and so on. In organizations, change storms arise with new management, mergers, and downsizing. In software, in can mean the introduction of many new competing platforms, where the eventual winner is far from certain.

4.3.3 Soft Forms

Sun Tzu's six key methods regarding space that is dominated by non-supporting features.

"You may have to move across marshes.
Move through them quickly without stopping."
Sun Tzu's The Art of War 9:1:15-16

"We sail within a vast sphere, ever drifting in
uncertainty, driven from end to end."
Blaise Pascal

General Principle: Soft opportunities can be used only as transitional positions.

Situation:

Soft ground offers us little solid support. Sun Tzu's analogy for soft ground is marsh land. Soft terrain can seem appealing as an opportunity because no one holds a position on it, so it seems empty. However, it is open for a reason: it cannot support anyone over time. These areas tend to swallow those that try to use them. They are characterized by uncertainty, a lack of solidity, and limited visibility. On this ground, we tend to get bogged down because the ground does not support a position. Their uncertainty is different from the normal limitations on our knowledge, known as "the fog of war." Here, what we are uncertain about is how well the ground will support us. We cannot get a good fix on our position.

Opportunity:

If we choose our opportunities correctly, each position works as a stepping stone to the next. Even though we cannot hold a long-standing position of soft ground, we can use these positions as transitional position. We learn how to recognize and use their uncertainty as a shortcut from one longer term position to another. We can get a relative advantage on this ground, using our relatively better knowledge against our opposition. In moving through these uncertain situations, we must avoid straying from our path and losing the traction we need to maintain our progress. When we master the skills of dealing with opportunities on soft ground, our probability of success improves dramatically.

Key Methods:

The key methods for recognizing and utilizing soft forms of ground are below.

1. On soft ground, the gravity of uncertain opinions tends to bog us down. On tilted ground, gravity is the tilt of opinion. On fluid ground, currents are determined by the direction of change. On soft ground, it is the opinions that are soft, changing direction under pressure. The opinions on soft ground cave under pressure. This ground offers the poorest information giving us the poorest ability to predict the future (2.1.1 Information Limits).

2. On soft ground, most existing positions are uncertain. In the psychological space of modern competition, soft opportunities are characterized by a lack of the key areas of support that we need to develop a permanent position. Perhaps the most common soft forms of ground shaped by our own indecision or the indecision of others (2.1.2 Leveraging Uncertainty).

3. This lack of support can take five forms. Soft forms of ground are defined by the following problems:

- A lack of physical resources (2.4.1 Ground Perspective)
- A lack of temporal resources (2.4.2 Climate Perspective)
- A lack of decisive character (2.4.3 Command Perspective)
- A lack of skills and systems (2.4.4 Methods Perspective)
- A lack of shared motivations (2.4.5 Mission Perspective t)

4. Soft opportunities are only _transitional_ positions. We can only use them as an intermediate step as part of a longer campaign. We use them to move from our current position to another desired position. Of course, all positions are temporary since all positions degrade over time, but soft positions can never truly support us and can only be used for transition (1.1.1 Position Dynamics).

5. We must only pursue soft opportunities when there are no alternative paths. Given their dangers, we pursue these transitional opportunities only when they are necessary to get from where we are to where we desire to be. If an alternative path that avoids soft ground is available, we should always use it (6.2 Campaigns).

6. We cannot stop moving on soft ground. This is the opposite of how we respond during a change storm on fluid forms of ground. On fluid ground, we stop and wait for the environment to stabilize (4.3.2 Fluid Forms), but on soft ground, we cannot stop. We get trapped in **indecision bogs** if we stop moving. Indecision bogs are more dangerous than change storms because they are more difficult to identify. Storms are noisy, disruptive, uncontrollable, and hard to miss. Bogs are quiet and serene on the surface. They wait so patiently to suck us in. Getting trapped on soft ground is often excused as "keeping our options open." We cannot leave critical decisions unresolved for long periods of time (3.1.6 Time Limitations).

7. When challenged, we must find the most solid ground available within these soft areas. These area lack some forms of key support, but they don't lack all support. We must identify which of the five key resources of ground, climate, character, methods, or mission are the most abundant. Only then can we get the most out of them, converting them into the resources that we lack (8.1.1 Transforming Resources).

Illustration:

It is a lot easier to understand soft forms of ground through a couple of illustrations from personal relationships and our professional career.

1. On soft ground, the gravity of uncertain opinions tends to bog us down. Two common examples are a) personal relationship in which a couple cannot decide to commit to marriage or not, and 2) spending time in college which is a preamble to starting our real career.

2. This lack of support can take five forms. Soft personal relations are a problem when we cannot decide to break up or go forward (lack of command support). If we get bogged down in these soft relationships, they can waste literally years of our their lives without developing our personal life. The same is true of time in college when we lack a mission or spend time getting an education without developing any real skills.

3. Soft opportunities are only _transitional_ positions. Soft romantic relations are transitional to finding permanent commitment. Going to college is another classical example of a transitional soft opportunity. Going to college does not support us financially (lack of ground support), instead it costs us. We go through college to get a degree to help us in our careers, but many people get bogged down in college, ending up wasting years of their life there and, too often, end up graduating with a degree that has little or no value in their career.

4. We must only pursue soft opportunities when there are no alternative paths. All romantic relationships start out as soft situations. We cannot know beforehand if the person is right for us. People get into these relationships with the goal of finding a permanent relationship. Many types of careers demand a college degree.

5. ***We cannot stop moving on soft ground***. Couples who live together but do not marry are making this mistake. Young people who attend college but never graduate are another.

6. ***When challenged, we must find the most solid ground available within these soft areas.*** In college, this means taking courses that have solid value in the marketplace. People are more likely to get through college studying something like science and business than they are something soft such as liberal arts. In relationships, this means setting deadlines for making decisions.

4.3.4 Neutral Forms

Sun Tzu's seven key methods for evaluating opportunities with no dominant ground form.

> *"On a level plateau, take a position that you can change."*
>
> Sun Tzu's The Art of War 9:1:22

> *"But some fell into good ground, and brought forth fruit, some an hundredfold, some sixtyfold, some thirtyfold."*
>
> Mat 13:8

General Principle: Neutral competitive ground forms offer the broadest range of potential positions.

Situation:

When the ground has a distinctive form, we can know where its advantages and disadvantages are. Form is a valuable key for evaluating the potential of opportunities. When a given ground lacks a distinctive form, it is more difficult to know where its advantages and disadvantages lie. We have clear principles for how to evaluate and pursue opportunities on unequal, fast-changing, and uncertain ground. When the ground lacks any of these forms, we need a different set of key methods. There is a danger in using the same rules for evaluating form on less distinguished ground.

Opportunity:

Neutral ground is the most flexible form of ground for competition. Since Sun Tzu's system is based on our ability to adapt to situations, this form of ground gives us the most options. Unequal, fast-changing, and uncertain ground are dominated by forces that may give some positions an inherent advantage over others. We leverage the nature of the ground to our advantage. We can filter out opportunities that put us in a disadvantageous position of these forms of ground. On neutral ground, there a more types of advantageous positions. In many ways, it is the ideal ground for competition, but we still need to understand the principles for best utilizing it.

Key Methods:

We need to understand the following key methods to best utilize neutral ground.

1. Neutral ground is relatively flat, stable, and solid. The advantages and disadvantages of tilted, fluid, and soft ground are relatively unimportant on neutral ground. The force of form--the gravity of inequality, the currents of change, and the uncertainty of support--are always present, but on neutral ground they are not strong enough to become a dominate factor in our decision about the quality of an opportunity (1.3.1 Competitive Comparison).

2. Neutral ground is not simply a combination of other forms of ground. Ground forms in combination are more complicated than neutral ground. A combination of factors makes it more difficult to identify high-probability opportunities. The competing forces involved are difficult to gauge accurately and the best decision is to avoid complex ground. Neutral ground is the opposite of complex ground. On neutral ground, these forces are mostly irrelevant (4.2 Choosing Non-Action). *Gravity still exists on neutral ground but it is not decisive.* Few competitive arenas are completely flat. Gravity, both physical and social, is always subtlety in play. The gravity of opinions may carry a little more weight in one direction than another but other factors are more important. We want to satisfy a broad range of opinions rather than a specific one. Though broad opinions are much less passionate than specific ones, we still want to hold the high ground, when we can find it (4.3.1 Tilted Forms).

3. Neutral ground does not have powerful, dominant currents. It may have seasonal cycles of change, and change may drift in one direction or another, but those eddying currents have a tendency to even out over time (4.3.2 Fluid Forms).

4. We can see and trust our footing on neutral ground. Neutral ground can support us. While our information is always limited in competitive situations, we can be relatively certain of our standing. We always want to choose positions where our information is the most solid, but this advantage is limited (4.3.3 Soft Forms).

5. On neutral ground, distance and dimension are more important than form. This makes neutral ground opportunities more appealing than those on the three other forms of ground. Neutral ground is a level playing field. Worrying only about distance and dimension makes these opportunities simpler and easier to evaluate (4.4 Strategic Distance , 4.5 Opportunity Surfaces).

6. The best positions on neutral ground are those that we can easily change. The best opportunities are those that lead to such positions. We always want positions that we can adapt to changing conditions, but this is more important on neutral ground because this form of ground offers more freedom of movement. The shape of other forms of ground constrain our movements (1.8.2 The Adaptive Loop).

Illustration:

Let us use the grocery store to demonstrate the characteristics of a ideal form of market.

1. Neutral ground is relatively flat, stable, and solid. Most of the products that we see in the grocery store are on neutral ground.

They are aimed at the average consumer. The brands involved do not change dramatically from year to year. The consumer product market provides solid financial support for these brands.

2. Neutral ground is _not_ simply a combination of other forms of ground. A good example of combination ground would be the music market. This market is not neutral, but very tilted because a few large companies and big artists have traditionally determined music popularity, distribution, and radio play. It is also fluid, because it is in transition from physical distribution, where people buy CDs, to electronic distribution. It is soft, because the market doesn't support most musicians. This combination makes it nearly impossible to identify a high-probability opportunity in the music market. Even winning on American Idol is not a guarantee of success.

3. Gravity still exists on neutral ground but it is not decisive. At the grocery store, it doesn't hurt to have the Good Housekeeping Seal of Approval, but it doesn't determine any products success or failure.

4. Neutral ground does not have powerful, dominant currents. In the grocery store, at various times, tastes may drift over time say, between smooth or chunky styles of peanut butter, but overall, the market is stable.

5. We can see and trust our footing on neutral ground. Milk, eggs, and all the rest of the products in the grocery store can depend on solid financial and cultural support as long as they maintain their position.

6. On neutral ground, distance and dimension are more important than form. How the competing grocery store brands do in the market have more to do with how convenient they are to buy and how well they are entrenched in the three opportunity dimensions of area, barriers, and stickiness.

7. The best positions on neutral ground are those that we can easily change. What is the most common message on packages in the grocery store? New and Improved. Most brands take positions that they can easily change. Some, such as Coca Cola, with its New Coke, found they weren't in such a position.

4.4 Strategic Distance

Sun Tzu's nine key methods regarding relative proximity in strategic space.

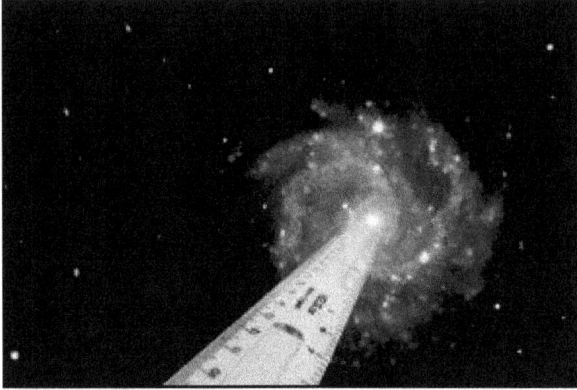

"The ground determines the distance.
The distance determines your numbers."
Sun Tzu's The Art of War 4:4:10-11

"If a man take no thought about what is distant, he will
find sorrow near at hand."
Confucius

General Principle: The greater its distance, the less the value of an opportunity.

Situation:

There is a danger hidden in improved communication. While improved communication is incredibly valuable, it means that we can hear about opportunities from anywhere in the world. This fact can lure us into the dangerous strategic error of thinking that distance no longer matters in choosing our opportunities. There are two mistakes in this thinking. First, it assumes that distance is simply a physical measure of space. Second, it assumes the communication alone eliminates the problems of distance.

Opportunity:

In picking high-probability opportunities, one of the most important characteristics is distance (4.0 Leveraging Probability). The further a new position is from our current position, the lower the probability of successfully moving to it directly. In a single lifetime, people can advance their position unbelievable distances, but those advances are made one step at a time. We pick close-by opportunities for the same reason we climb up stairs instead of leaping to the top of buildings in a single bound. Smaller moves are easier and much more likely to be successful.

Key Methods:

While everyone instinctively recognizes the importance of distance, the Warrior's Rules regarding distance are sophisticated, covering many aspects of distance that are easily overlooked.

1. Distance is both physical and intellectual. Distance always measures space, but there is objective space and subjective space. Physical space and intellectual space both contain distance. ___Distance___ describes the differences in space and knowledge *separating* two positions. We must move over distance to get from one position to another. We can be physically close and intellectually close in different ways. This stems from the objective and subjective nature of positions (1.2 Subobjective Positions).

2. Closer openings are always better than more distant ones. In choosing the best opportunities, we must make a simple comparison of distance. Openings that contain or create more distance are never as good as the alternatives that contain or create more closeness (5.5.2 Distance Limitations).

3. Both physical and intellectual distance are measured in differences. These two types of distance are different, just as the subjective and objective positions are different. We can be physically close to someone without being intellectually close to them. We can be intellectually close without being physically close. Distance measures a degree of difference. In space, we can measure it in feet and miles, meters and kilometers. Intellectual distance measures the differences in knowledge and perspective (1.3.1 Competitive Comparison).

4. *Both distance from our current position and distance from people decrease success probability*. Successful moves are more likely in the short-term if they keep close to our current position. They are also more likely to succeed in the long term if they bring us closer to more people. Opportunities close to where we are are more probably successful than those further away. Opportunities that bring us closer to more people are more probably successful (4.0 Leveraging Probability.

5. *Proximity is physical closeness, the opposite of physical distance*. Originally, the concept of "being at the right place at the right time" was focused on physical location. The more people we are close to, the easier it is to make connections and the more successful we are. (4.4.1 Physical Distance).

6. *Physical proximity increases our probability of success*. In searching for proximity to other people, people move from the country to cities and from small cities to large ones. Large organizations are housed in large office buildings, complexes, and campuses because physical proximity is valuable. People in cities and office buildings all enjoyed the strategic advantage of being close to each other. People who were close to others are generally more successful to people than people whose positions enjoyed fewer advantages of proximity (2.6 Knowledge Leverage).

7. *Affinity is intellectual closeness, the opposite of intellectual distance.* In the mental landscape, we are further away from those with different goals, different views of the future, different skills, and different personalities. A personal affinity for a position makes it intellectually attractive. This is based on a feeling of identification with that position. Affinity leads to connection among people of similar interests. It can mean a similarity in positions, but it less often means identical positions than it does compatible or, more to the point, complementary positions (4.4.2 Intellectual Distance).

8. *Affinity is growing more important in determining success*. Proximity is still very important, but because of technological change, affinity is becoming more important. Advances in transportation and especially communication have decreased the impact of physical proximity. The growing access of people everywhere to a wider variety of alternatives is making *affinity* increasingly more important. Because of all the new forms of communication and transportation, people are connecting with others more and more on the basis of their affinities, the intellectual and emotional closeness that they share. The challenge in evaluating opportunities is the changing nature of distance in the world today as physical distance becomes less important and intellectual and emotional distance becomes more important ((1.4.1 Climate Shift).

9. *Physical and intellectual distance can create each other over time*. This is just like subjective and objective positions creating each other as complementary opposites.When we are physically close to people, we tend to get intellectually closer. If we are intellectually close to people, we want to get physically closer. The reverse is also true. If we are physically distant over time, we will become more intellectual distant (3.2.3 Complementary Opposites).

Illustration:

Let us look at how we can use these key methods to evaluate different job opportunities.

1. *Distance is both physical and intellectual*. A job opportunity that requires us to master more new skills is less likely than one that requires us to master fewer new skills.

2. *Closer openings are always better than more distant ones*. A job opportunity that requires us to move a great distance is never as good as one that doesn't.

3. *Both physical and intellectual distance are measured in differences*. A job opportunity that associates us with people with whom we have little in common is worse than one that associates us with people with whom we have more in common.

4. *Both distance from our current position and distance from people decrease success probability*. A job that isolates us from contact with people is less likely to bring success than one that puts us in contact with many people.

5. *Proximity is physical closeness, the opposite of physical distance*. Jobs that improve our proximity to those whose decisions affect our future are better than those that distance us from those people.

6. *Physical proximity increases our probability of success*. A job opportunity that requires a long daily commute is not as good as one that doesn't.

7. *Affinity is intellectual closeness, the opposite of intellectual distance.* Jobs that put us in contact with those with whom we share many things are better than those that put us in contact with those with whom we share little.

8. *Affinity is growing more important in determining success*. More and more businesses are being shaped by their ability to attract people with a similar mindset as well as needed skills.

9. *Physical and psychological distance can create each other over time.* Over the long term, we will tend to share the thinking of those with whom we work and tend to physically get together with those with whom we share our thinking.

4.4.1 Physical Distance

Sun Tzu's six key methods regarding the issues of proximity in physical space.

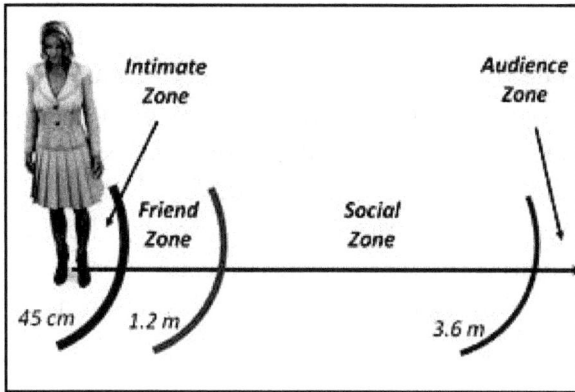

> *"You must analyze the obstacles, dangers, and distances.
> This is the best way to command."*
> Sun Tzu's The Art of War 10:3:4-5

> *"Distance lends enchantment to the view."*
> Mark Twain

General Principle: : The greater its distance, the less the value of an opportunity.

Situation:

Space: the final frontier. We can explore more space, but does broadening our activities uncover better opportunities? Going greater distances certainly increases our costs. The mistake is thinking that it automatically increase our rewards. The grass may look greener on the other side of the fence, but is that an illusion? The rewards of any opportunity are impossible to know before exploring it. Distant opportunities often seem bigger just because of a trick of perspective. Such opportunities are exotic and different, but that fact makes them more risky as opposed to more certain.

Opportunity:

We can use physical distance to prioritize opportunities. Physical distance is easy to compare (1.3.1 Competitive Comparison). We know for certain that a move from New York to New Jersey is shorter than a move from New York to California. In picking the best opportunities, we look for small movement in physical space that can dramatically improve our position. Remember, to advance our position, we must make only profitable moves. This means we must think about the cost of each move. Among these costs is cycle time because increasing distance also creates increases in the time it takes us to get feedback on the effectiveness of our activities (1.8.3 Cycle Time).

Key Methods:

Sun Tzu offers the following six key methods related to physical distance.

1. Production is duplicated over physical distance more easily than competitive strategy. The problems with physical distance are a matter of external differences. Competition depends much more on external conditions than production systems, which rely more on internal organizations. The central problem with physical distance is getting good local information about dynamic, external condition, which vary widely from region to region (<u>1.9 Competition and Production</u>).

2. Leadership is always local because it cannot be projected over physical distance. Someone must take the responsibility to make decisions on the spot. Leaders must see and be seen to understand the situation. This is often done by <u>gut decisions</u> that unconsciously process more information than we can put into words. Communication doesn't replace physical presence. Physical presence always provides better information than communication systems. Strategy depends on oneon-one relationships and those relationships are impossible to develop and maintain given physical separation. Our contact networks in remote places are never going to be as complete or reliable as local ones (2.3 Personal Interactions).

3. *Physical distance is always costly to navigate.* The higher our costs, the lower our likelihood of success. High-probability opportunities include a minimum of costly distance. Physical Distance necessitates two forms of costs. ***Transportation costs*** are the costs created by moving between places. Communication costs are the costs of communication. Strategy depends upon making moves that pay and the higher the costs, the less probably it is that given more will pay (3.1.2 Strategic Profitability).

4. *The costs of physical distance can be mitigated but not eliminated.* While modern technology has dramatically reduced the physical cost of transportation and communication, it cannot eliminate those costs. Even in an era of instant communication, we do not eliminate the differences in time zone or language that are part of physical distance. Those difference create many different costs, including the frequency of errors and the cycle time needed to correct such errors. The further we have to travel to take advantage of an opportunity, the more costly it will be to pursue that opportunity (4.4 Strategic Distance).

5. *Separation over physical distance can lead to separation of goals.* Shared goals hold organizations together. The larger organizations are, the more difficult it is to maintain common goals. Size is not always a matter of number of people. It is always a function of the physical distance separating those people (3.4 Dis-Economies of Scale).

6. ***The best moves forward are always local ones, covering only a minimum of physical distance.*** We must learn to prefer opportunities that are physically close to where we are now. When we pick actions with which we explore an opportunity, we want to pick the closest moves, but this philosophy must start with picking the right opportunities (5.5.2 Distance Limitations).

Illustration:

Consider the challenge of opening new sales offices in distant locations.

*7. **Production is duplicated over physical distance more easily than competitive strategy.*** Opening remote hamburger stands, which are production locations, is much easier than opening remote sales offices.

*8. **Leadership is always local because it cannot be projected over physical distance.*** At each local sales office, an individual must take responsibility for making it work. That individual must learn from someone with more experience about how to make those decisions. That means that he must be transferred there, trained by someone on site a period of time, or move someone else for training for a period of time.

*9. **Physical distance is always costly to navigate.*** When we have opened new distant sales offices, we are going to have to spend more money to operating them than ones that are closer to us. The transfer and training described above is just the start. So these offices are always going to be less profitable over time.

*10. **The costs of physical distance can be mitigated but not eliminated.*** New technology, such as video conferencing, help, but do not eliminate the problem with leadership, management, and creating relationships.

*11.**Separation over physical distance can lead to separation of goals.*** People in different sales offices are going to develop different goals depending on their local conditions.

*12. **The best moves forward are always local ones, covering only a minimum of physical distance.*** Local salespeople are always going to have a higher probability of success than distant ones.

4.4.2 Intellectual Distance

Sun Tzu's six key methods regarding the challenges of moving through intellectual space.

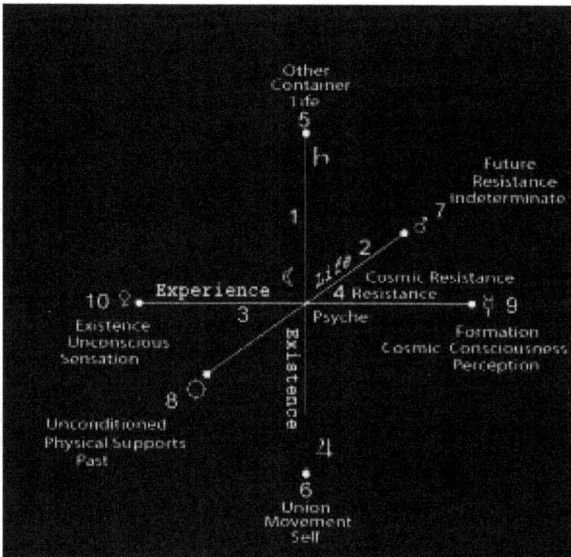

"You can be close to an ally and still part ways."
Sun Tzu's The Art of War 1:4:14

"The most painful thing about mathematics is how far away you are from being able to use it after you have learned it."

James Newman

General Principle: The best opportunities are those that pay off with the least new learning.

Situation:

The less we know about an opportunity, the better it looks. This is a central challenge when picking high-probability opportunities.

The challenge is worse in this new era of communication, where intellectual distance seems to be minimized by our communication systems. Unlike physical proximity, intellectual affiliations and differences are difficult to identify, quantify, and compare. Intellectual closeness and distance are much more varied and complex than physical closeness. People that are intellectually close in some areas of affinity can be very distant than others. Unity based on affinity and opposed to proximity is relatively fragile and tentative.

Opportunity:

The intellectual terrain has always been more important than the physical terrain in strategic competition. It also offers many more opportunities. Those who understand the principles of intellectual distance have a tremendous advantage in our more competitive world.Gauging intellectual distance is more difficult than physical difference, but it can be simplified by a single concept: learning. Just as travel covers physical distance, learning covers intellectual distance. Distance is a measure of differences (4.4 Strategic Distance). Our differences in goals, attitude, knowledge, character, and skills make up intellectual distance (1.3 Elemental Analysis). The more learning pursuing a given opportunity requires, the more distant it is from our current location.

Key Methods:

The key methods regarding intellectual distance are perhaps even more fundamental than those regarding physical distance.

1. All strategic moves to a new position require learning to cross intellectual distances. While a given strategic move to a new position may or may not require a physical move to a new location, they always require mastering new knowledge. We may not travel physical distance, but we must work to travel intellectual distance. It is measured in how much work we must do to get from one intellectual place to another. This learning is a measure of effort and time, in the same way that traveling physical distance is measured in effort and time. (2.6 Knowledge Leverage).

2. We can travel intellectual distance in the five elemental dimensions. The dimensions of mission, climate, ground, command, and methods represent five different types of learning. We can "move" by learning 1) new motivations, 2) new trends of change, 3) new competitive arenas--their players and rules, 4) new people, and 5) new skills and systems (1.3 Elemental Analysis).

3. Learning to navigate intellectual distance requires investment. The higher these costs, the lower our likely success. High-probability opportunities include a minimum of costly distance. Intellectual distance necessitates two forms of costs. **Communication** costs are the investments needed to acquire new knowledge. Learning costs are the investments required to integrate that knowledge into our decision-making. Strategy depends upon making moves that pay and the higher the costs, the less probable it is that given move will pay (3.1.2 Strategic Profitability).

4. These costs of covering intellectual distance can be mitigated but not eliminated. While modern technology has dramatically reduced the cost of communication, it cannot eliminate the cost of learning. No matter how available the information, it requires time and effort to integrate it into our decision-making. This costs including the frequency of our errors and the cycle time needed to correct such errors. The more we have to learn to take advantage of an opportunity, the more costly it will be to pursue that opportunity (4.4 Strategic Distance).

5. Organizations must learn together to stay united when crossing intellectual distances. Shared goals hold organizations together. The larger organizations are, the more difficult it is to maintain common goals. Size is not always a matter of number of people. It is always a function of the differences in their knowledge levels. Different knowledge creates different perspectives and goals, which divide organizations (3.4 Dis-Economies of Scale).

6. The best moves forward reuse existing knowledge to minimize the crossing intellectual distances. In other words, we try to minimize learning. We must prefer opportunities that are intellectually close to where we are now. When we pick actions with which we explore an opportunity, we want to pick those which are mostly familiar to us (5.5.2 Distance Limitations).

Illustration:

As an illustration of these principles, let us think about our careers and how we pursue them both within and without organizations.

1. All strategic moves to a new position require learning to cross intellectual distances. An individual once had to rely upon a position within an organization--a position in the mental landscape not the physical one--for his or her situation. Moves up in the organization require learning a little broader area of responsibility. However,

2. We can travel intellectual distance in the five elemental dimensions. For example, any move from one job to another entails a change in climate, a change in command, and changes in systems. Moving from a job as an assembly line worker to a sales job is a bigger change than moving from selling to one group of customers to selling to different customers because it requires more learning.

3. Learning to navigate intellectual distance requires investment. Because of limitations in learning, people's options are limited in terms of pursuing opportunities. Many, perhaps most, once aspired to stay with the same organization their entire career, moving up the corporate ladder rather than striking out on their own because of the loss of affinity, the shared knowledge within the organization. This strengthened the competitive position of organizations, but it weakened the competitive position of individuals. The factory town was the hallmark of individuals being trapped by an organization using proximity, which is physical closeness, and affinity, which is intellectual closeness.

4. These costs of covering intellectual distance can be mitigated but not eliminated. Individuals are increasingly freed from their dependence on organizations for their career positions by improved communication. Using telecommuting, people can work anywhere in the world, associating with others in the value chain based upon their personal as opposed to organizational knowledge. Using on-line shopping, people can buy products anywhere in the world. However, the knowledge of any one person is still limited, even with access to the internet. A formal organization still has a more diverse set of intellectual skills than a single individual.

5. *Organizations must learn together to stay united when crossing intellectual distances.* The concept of the corporation was built on minimizing intellectual distance: a group of people working together toward a shared goal develop an affinity for each other. Today, we are seeing all types of groups form around all types of affinities, shared forms of caring, in cyberspace. This means that individuals must learn and master more strategic skills to navigate the challenges of the new world order. Organizations at every level, business and state, provide less and less protection from competitive pressure. Longer term, this shifts the strategic balance to individuals who develop strategic skills and, based on those skills, position themselves at the future crossroads of opportunity.

6. *The best moves forward reuse existing knowledge to minimize the crossing intellectual distances.* Home isn't just a physical location, but an intellectual place. As the saying goes, "Home is where the heart is." One of the fundamental changes underlying our current financial crisis it that organizations no longer enjoy the competitive benefits of exclusive affinity among people that they once did. The advantage is shifting from organizations at every level to individuals. We see this in every competitive arena from sports to politics, the competitive issues are less about the organizational affinity and more about the individual affinity.

4.5 Opportunity Surfaces

Sun Tzu's six key methods on judging potential opportunities from a distance.

"You must analyze the obstacles, dangers, and distances. This is the best way to command."

Sun Tzu's The Art of War 1:4:14

"It is easier to perceive error than to find truth, for the former lies on the surface and is easily seen, while the latter lies in the depth, where few are willing to search for it."

Johann Wolfgang von Goethe

General Principle: The surface characteristics of an opportunity are their area, barriers, and holding power.

Situation:

To pick high-probability opportunities, we must make judgments from a distance before investing in the opportunity. We eliminate the most distant opportunities because we cannot see them clearly.

We are warned not to judge a book by its cover, but we must judge opportunities by their surface characteristics. We want to conserve our resources by pursuing our best opportunities. We need tools to help us determine which opportunities are likely to be best.

Opportunity:

Sun Tzu's strategy is the science of what happens on the front-lines, on the boundaries, where one person or organization makes contact with the outside world. Using a living cell as an analogy, strategy is not the programmed instructions of the cell's DNA. It is the interactive process on the surface of the cell, the cell's membrane that adapts to external conditions from moment to moment. When it comes to judging opportunities, the surface is particularly important. From a distance, we can only see the surface of an opportunity. While the value of an opportunity may, like gold, be buried deeply in an opportunity, the most common problems are right on the surface if we know how to look. Our ability to choose the best possible opportunities depends on our ability to eliminate opportunity surfaces that can prevent our progress now and in the future (1.1 Position Paths).

Key Methods:

The following key methods describe the key surface characteristics of an opportunity and how we use it.

1. We can make decisions about surface characteristics from a distance. Distance describes the differences **separating** two positions. We cannot know the true value of opportunity without making a move to explore the depth of the opportunity. We can only see it from a distance. What we see from a distance is just its surface, so we must make our judgments based on that surface (3.1.5 Unpredictable Value).

2. We can observe three surface characteristics called area, barriers, and holding power. Strategic area describes the amount of surface. Barriers describes the roughness of a surface. Stickiness describes the holding power of a surface. We have to examine three of the surface characteristics to eliminate the worst opportunities. These characteristics tell us a great deal about the future potential of an opportunity (4.1 Future Potential).

3. *Area describes the amount of surface that must be covered.* Area measures the breadth and range that a future position encompasses. Area describes the differences in space and knowledge *within* a given position. A position can attempt to control a small or broad territory. The more area in a strategic surface, the broader the space and/or knowledge that must be mastered to take advantage of that opportunity. This can be either an advantage or disadvantage depending on the specifics of our situation (4.5.1 Opportunity Area).

4. *Barriers describes the roughness of a surface.* Barriers refer to the number of obstacles encountered in moving from one position to another. Think of these obstacles as "barriers to entry." In physical space, these obstacles can have a number of different forms: differences in elevation, depth of water, and uncertain footing. In intellectual space, these translated into the knowledge barriers: hierarchies, change, and uncertainty. The more barriers around a certain opportunity, the more specialized and rare the skills and resources required to navigate that surface. While more area requires more resources, more barriers require not only more resources but specific types of skills and resources. Barriers create strategic spaces that are easy to defend but difficult to advance (4.5.2 Opportunity Barriers).

5. *Holding power describes the stickiness or slipperiness of a surface.* This is the most complicated characteristic of a strategic opportunity. Sun Tzu described it as "dangers" because this characteristic in holding an occupant prevents movement and progress. The lack of holding power, slipperiness, is also a problem since it makes holding a position difficult. In the mental landscape, holding power is often determined by how strongly a position is understood and remembered versus how easily it is confused and forgotten. Both sticky and slippery spaces are easy to defend and difficult to advance but for very different reasons (4.5.3 Opportunity Holding Power).

6. Surface characteristics allow us to eliminate the problematic opportunities. As we study these characteristics, we discover that, unlike distance, these characteristics are neither simply good or bad, but they do determine both the limitations and potential of different opportunities. More or less surface area, barriers, and holding power have very different affects on our ability to make progress using a given opportunity. They affect all three aspects of progress, our ability to 1) advance into a position, 2) defending that position while we hold it, and 3) advance from that position in the future. (4.4 Strategic Distance).

7. Surface characteristics can mislead us about the potential of opportunities. Many of the principles describing the advantages and disadvantages of these three characteristics are non-intuitive. Advantages that make it easy to get into a position can turn to disadvantages when it comes time to move on from that position. Without knowing these principles, we can see "obvious" advantages and easily miss the more subtle disadvantages (4.1 Future Potential).

Illustration:

For an illustration, let us imagine that we have a chain of retail stores and are evaluating various rental location for opening a new store.

1. We can make decisions about surface characteristics from a distance. We can know that location is the key, but we cannot know the true potential of a location before we open the store.

2. We can observe three surface characteristics called area, barriers, and holding power. In evaluating potential locations, we can only observe these three characteristics if we ask and consider them.

3. Area describes the amount of surface that must be covered. We can evaluate the size of potential in a variety of ways. How big a community does a location serve? How distant are the nearest direct competitors? How busy is the location in terms of existing traffic? Does the size of the retail space meet our needs?

4. *Barriers describes the roughness of a surface.* How much remodeling does the space require? How easy is it to obtain local licenses and permits? How easy will it be to negotiate a reasonable rental rate in the area?

5. *Holding power describes the stickiness or slipperiness of a surface.* How long a lease are we obligated to? If the store fails, can we get out? How easily can we expand at the location? If the store succeeds, can we grow? What happens to the rental rates over time?

6. *Surface characteristics allow us to quickly eliminate the problematic opportunities.* Where do the excess or lack of these qualities create problems or costs in moving into the location, adapting it over time, and moving out of it in the future.

7. *Surface characteristics can mislead us about the potential of opportunities.* Some characteristics will make it easy to move in but hard to move out. Others will make the position easier or more difficult to keep the store profitable over time.

4.5.1 Surface Area

Sun Tzu's seven key methods for choosing opportunities on the basis of their size.

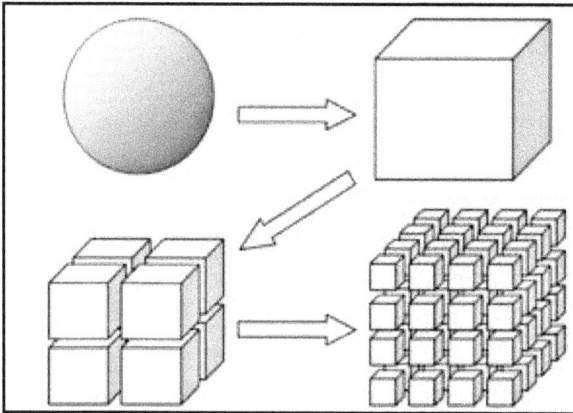

"Victory comes from correctly using both large and small forces."

Sun Tzu's The Art of War 3:5:3

"So never lose an opportunity of urging a practical beginning, however small, for it is wonderful how often in such matters the mustard-seed germinates and roots itself."

Florence Nightingale

General Principle: Large and small opportunities offer very different types of advantages.

Situation:

Surface area measures the apparent size of an opportunity. We mistakenly think that the bigger the opportunity, the more likely it is to lead to success. However, the advantages coming from the size of an opportunity can be very misleading. We think that we need a "big break" to be successful. We think that big breaks depend solely upon luck. However, the advantages of big opportunities often disguise extremely costly dangers. We can easily mistake the size of the territory in which the opportunity arises for the space within the opportunity itself.

Opportunity:

As we learn more about gauging the size of an opportunity, picking high-opportunity opportunities become much easier. Once we understand what the "size" on an opportunity really means, we can gauge how well a given opportunity fits our unique abilities to utilize it (3.4.2 Opportunity Fit). With the right perspective on opportunity size, we avoid costly mistakes regarding picking opportunities that seem closer than they are because of their size (4.4 Strategic Distance). One of the most important ways we benchmark opportunities is identifying those that are too spread out and those that are too confined (4.6.1 Extremes of Area).

Key Methods:

Below are the key methods that describe the use of opportunity area in comparing the potential of opportunities.

1. Opportunity area is different from opportunity distance. Opportunity area evaluates the breadth and range of territory that a future position encompasses. The space covered by position is different from that separating positions. Area is the extent, range, or and capacity ***within*** an opportunity, the expanse of the region it covers. Distance is the space ***separating*** different positions, the investment that must be made to explore an opportunity from an existing position. Opportunity area contains and covers distance to the extent that opportunities exist as opening between existing positions. Area and distance are similar, existing both in physical and intellectual space and measured in differences. (4.4 Strategic Distance).

2. Opportunity area measures the range of physical and intellectual capacities. Positions exist both on physical and mental landscapes. We can measure physical area in the feet and miles, meters and kilometers an opportunity covers. We measure intellectual area in the range of knowledge and skills an opportunity requires to address. An opportunity is an opening and physical space and intellectual space both measure the extent or capacity of that opening. These two aspects of area stem from the dual objective and subjective nature of positions (1.2 Objective and Subjective Positions).

3. The area of the competitive landscape is measured by the number of optional positions available. Since a position is a combination of the characteristics of mission, climate, ground, command, and methods, potential positions on a competitive landscape is a combination of those characteristics. As the possible characteristics get multiplied together defining optional positions, this number of options grows very large. The area of an given opportunity or opening describes a small subset of the competitive landscape with a more limited number of combination of characteristics (1.3 Elemental Analysis).

4. The larger the opportunity area, the more resources required to fill it. We can often see the size of an opportunity more easily if we think about the resources required to pursue it. We explore opportunities with the excess resources that we do not need for maintaining our current position. Physical space must be traveled. Intellectual space must be covered. The larger the area, the more needs, time, materials, decisions, and skills that opportunity requires required to cover it. "Big" opportunity areas require more range and depth of resources than small opportunity areas (3.4.2 Opportunity Fit).

5. Small areas of opportunities are much more common than large ones. Opportunities are openings, often in the form of unsatisfied needs. The vast majority of opportunities exist as empty spaces between existing positions. The spaces between large competitors tend to be filled by smaller competitors and the spaces between those smaller competitors are what remain. This is why small openings are much more common than large ones. Large areas of opening only exist on the periphery of most existing positions, created as new areas of opportunity are opened up or created by new methods (3.2 Opportunity Creation).

6. Small opportunities can eventually lead to larger ones. Since opportunities are unmet needs, one unmet need can lead to another opportunity in a chain. Like following a vein of gold in a mine, small threads of opportunity can lead to gradually large, unrecognized areas of need. Working on the periphery of existing positions can lead to the periphery of all existing positions (3.7 Defining the Ground).

7. The larger the opportunity area, the more probably a partial fit becomes. Opportunities are openings that we can fill and needs that we can satisfy. Opportunities have a shape and size and our resources have a shape and size. The larger the area of an opportunity, the more likely it is that our available resources will fit part of that opportunity. Our resources are always limited (3.1.1 Resource Limitations).

8. Large and unfilled opportunities attract more competition. While all opportunities are difficult to see, larger opportunities are easier to see than small ones. Because of their size, they can be seen at a greater distance. Once we begin to fill an opening, it instantly becomes easier for others to see. Since larger opportunities are more difficult for us to fill, when we pursue large opportunities, we expose them to other potential competitors (3.2.2 Opportunity Invisibility).

Illustration:

Let us illustrate these principles discussing the choosing of a geographically large sales territory versus a smaller one. This is an interesting problem because salespeople often prefer large territories because they think that they hold more potential prospects.

1. Opportunity area is different from opportunity distance. The area a new sales territory covers is different from the distance it takes to get to that territory. Taking over a distant territory may require a commute or even moving to even get to it. Traveling within the territory is different than getting to it.

2. *Opportunity area measures the range of physical and intellectual capacities*. A geographically large territory may or may not contain more prospects but always contains more distance, the space between the prospect. A better measure for a sales territory is the population within it. Another way to measure the intellectual extent of a territory is the range of products that a salesperson must learn to represent or the number of different types of businesses he must address. Sales territory can also be measured in terms of the size of the customers it addresses. A geographically large territory can contain only a few large customers while a geographically small territory can contain a large number of small customers.

3. *The area of the competitive landscape is measured by the number of optional positions available.* The size of a sale territory can be measured by the physical territory it covers, by the number of prospects within it, by the number of different products sold within it, by the number of orders it generates, by its total sales volume, by the sales commission it generates, and on. While some of these characteristics may correlate with one another, others do not. For example, a territory that generates the most sales volume could have a few very large customers rather than the most customers.

4. *The larger the opportunity area, the more resources required to fill it.* It takes more time to cover a geographically or demographically large territory. The larger the territory, the less frequent the visits to potential prospects and existing customers. The more products and types of business a territory covers, the greater the range of sales knowledge that is required on the part of the salesperson.

5. *Small areas of opportunities are much more common than large ones.* As a market and company matures, sales territories tend to get whittled down, smaller and smaller. Large sales territories are more common in new, unproven companies and industries.

6. Small opportunities can eventually lead to larger ones. Success in a small territory can lead to a large one. Success in selling small customers can lead to selling large ones.

7. The larger the opportunity area, the more probably a partial fit becomes. Salespeople offering new technologies open up large areas of application. They tend to find more diverse areas of applications, most of which offer a partial solution and none of which offer a complete solution.

8. Large and unfilled opportunities attract more competition. If a given salesperson is successful selling to certain new markets, more salespeople will pursue that market. Many poorly fitting applications of new technology tend to attract those offering better fitting applications.

4.5.2 Surface Barriers

Seven key methods regarding how to select opportunities by evaluating obstacles.

"Everyone confronts these obstacles on a campaign."
Sun Tzu's The Art of War 11:1:30

"The greater the obstacle, the more glory in overcoming it."
Molier

General Principle: We must compare opportunities by the difficulty, number, and familiarity of their barriers.

Situation:

Barriers describes the difficulties in filling the opening presented by given opportunity. Barriers are obstacles that block our access to the opportunities. While opportunities are always difficult to see, opportunity barriers can be either readily apparent or nearly invisible. When apparent, these barriers can completely discourage us from pursuing high-probability opportunities. When barriers are difficult to see, they can lure us into pursuing opportunities that have a very poor chance of success.

Opportunity:

Without barriers, the openings that define opportunities would be quickly filled without our efforts. In other words, without barriers, the needs that create opportunities would not exist. The nature of a given opportunity's barriers separates our opportunities from opportunities best suited to others (3.4.2 Opportunity Fit). Like distance, barriers create a cost to pursuing an opportunity, but unlike distance, that cost is not determined by proximity but capability (4.4 Strategic Distance). Barriers can be good or bad depending how well they fit our capabilities. While they increase the costs in some aspects of using a given opportunity, they can also decrease those costs over time (4.6.2 Extremes of Barriers).

Key Methods:

The following key methods describe how to understand the nature of barriers in comparing our opportunities.

1. Opportunity barriers describe the physical and intellectual obstacles blocking an opening. In physical space, these obstacles can be differences in elevation, moving water, and soft ground. In intellectual space, we meet social barriers, knowledge barriers, personality barriers, changing trends and so on. Obstacles describe any surface condition making transition slower or more difficult (4.5 Surface Characteristics).

2. Barriers are measured in difficulty, number, and familiarity. We usually discuss the size of barriers in terms of how difficult or easy they are to surmount. A small barrier requires less effort or investment than a large one. A few large barriers can be much more of an obstacle than many small barriers. The wild-card is familiarity. The more familiar we are with a given type of barrier, the more we know whether it is easy or difficult to surmount (3.2.1 Environmental Dominance).

3. Probability of success is determined by internal resources as well as external conditions. The advantage or disadvantage comes from the specific nature of the barriers, our internal resources, and how our resources compare with those of potential competitors. The barriers and competitors are external conditions, but our resources are internal (4.6.2 Extremes of Barriers).

4. *The more barriers, the more costly it is to pursue an opportunity.* Costs are increased in both the time and money it takes to advance to the new position. The higher the costs, the less the reward so the larger the number of barriers, the less likely it is that the reward pays off (3.1 Strategic Economics).

5. *Barriers make it less costly to defend a position.* This is the defensive side of the equation. Positions blocked by barriers may be more expensive to win, but they are less expensive to defend (4.6.3 Barricaded Conditions).

6. *Advantages in overcoming barriers are a matter of resource fitness.* Surmounting barriers isn't just a matter of investment. Investing more doesn't guarantee success. Success is often a matter of having the right capabilities to surmount a particular type of barrier. If the barrier is a mountain, mountain climbing and equipment gives us the resources we need. If the barrier is a lake, having a boat is valuable. If the problem requires sales skills, sales resources are important. If it demands product development, development skills are important (3.1.1 Resource Limitations).

7. *Picking the best opportunity is a simple comparison of opportunity barriers and available resources.* While opportunity barriers can get very complicated if our goal was to thoroughly analyze them, fortunately, in actual practice, this is seldom necessary. Once we consider the barriers involved and the resources required, we should be able to see in a flash which opportunities fit our particular resources. If others have a better set of resources to meet the challenges of a particular opportunity, we should not pursue it (1.3.1 Competitive Comparison).

Illustration:

Let us consider the barriers in pursuing different careers.

1. Opportunity barriers describe the physical and intellectual obstacles blocking an opening. Learning means covering a lot of ground but that ground has few barriers, just about anyone can do it. As opposed to managing a fast-food franchise, becoming a nuclear scientist or a professional level athlete offers a host of barriers.

2. Barriers are measured in difficulty, number, and familiarity. There may be a lot of different tasks to learn in order to run a fast-food franchise, but none of those tasks are particularly difficult and most are familiar. The barriers to becoming a professional athlete are extremely difficult but familiar. In contrast, the barriers to becoming a nuclear scientist are both difficult and unfamiliar.

3. The more barriers, the more costly it is to pursue an opportunity. Working in a fast-food franchise is much less costly than starting one. The costs of pursuing a professional career are amplified by the low probability of success.

4. Barriers make it less costly to defend a position. A career in nuclear science or as a professional athlete is much easier to maintain than to establish. A fast-food franchise, however, is always facing new competition.

5. Probability of success is determined by internal resources as well as external conditions. Different people have different capabilities. For some people, doing what is necessary to run a fast food chain may be much more difficult than learning nuclear science or becoming an athlete

6. Advantages in overcoming barriers is a matter of resource fitness. The skills involved in becoming a nuclear scientist or a professional level athlete are extremely difficult to master and well beyond most people's capabilities. In the case of more professional athletes, those capabilities have a time limit as well.

7. Picking the best opportunity is a simple comparison of opportunity barriers and available resources. Even if we have the opportunity to become a professional athlete and some of the resources required, that opportunity has a lower probability of success because of the height of the barriers involved.

4.5.3 Surface Holding Power

Sun Tzu's seven key methods regarding sticky and slippery situations.

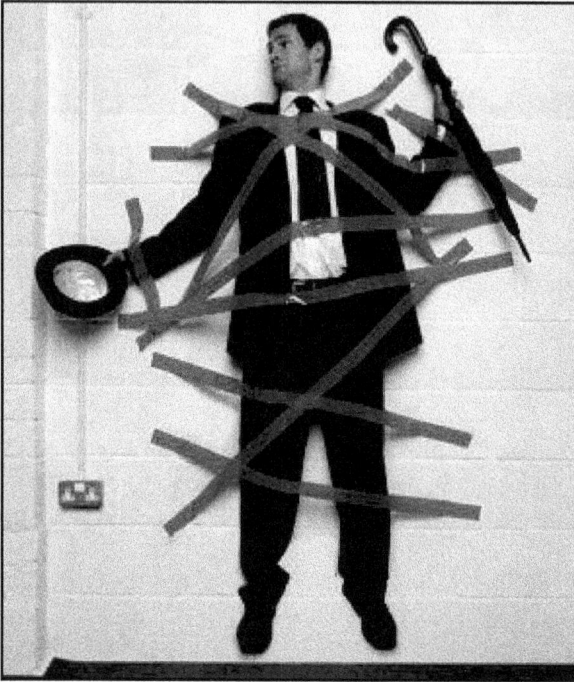

"You cannot leave some positions without losing an advantage."

Sun Tzu's The Art of War 10:1:24

"It keeps users engaged, so it keeps our site sticky. We've already turned browsers into buyers, and that's all that matters."

Meredith Medland

General Principle: Holding power makes positions easy to defend and hard to change.

Situation:

Some positions are sticky, making it difficult to move on from them. Others are slippery and very difficult to hold onto. When we are examining our opportunities, the relative holding power of a new position the most easily overlooked of all its characteristics. While misunderstandings about opportunity size and barriers are common, these characteristics are usually considered. This is not true for holding power, which is seldom considered at all. This is unfortunate because holding has tremendous influence on our probability of success both in using a position and moving on from it.

Opportunity:

Since holding power is so easily overlooked, understanding it gives us the ability to see more deeply into the nature of a position than others. More importantly, it enables us to avoid the problems associated with too much or too little holding power in a position (4.2 Choosing Non-Action). Understanding holding power also allows us to make better decisions about how to utilize a given opportunity as a stepping stone in making progress (1.1 Position Paths). As with all surface characteristics, mastering Sun Tzu's idea of holding power gives us a concrete concept that we can observe and evaluate before pursuing an opportunity.

Key Methods:

The following six key methods describe how to understand the value of holding powers in gauging different opportunities.

1. Holding power describes adhesion and repulsion of a potential position. Holding power is the strength of the connection between a position and its holder. In physical space, this holding power describes how sticky or slippery an area is. Sticky positions have a great deal of holding power so moving from them is costly in terms of resources. Slippery positions have very little holding power so keeping to them is costly. In intellectual space, these ideas translate into how concretely position is understood and sticks in the memory (4.5 Surface Characteristics).

2. *In more stable environments, holding power appears as friction*. When we describe holding power in terms of stickiness and slipperiness, we infer some fluidity to the ground. The antonym of both sticky and slippery is dry. Environments range from stable to fluid. In more fluid environments, change acts like lubrication. When opportunities lack fluidity, that is, when the ground is very stable, holding power appears as the presence of friction making the ground easier to hold but more costly to move out upon (4.3.2 Fluid Forms).

3. *An abundance of holding power makes it less costly to maintain a position*. The friction of holding power keeps values aligned, slows down events, makes resources more dependable, creates relationships among people, and stabilizes processes. Holding power makes positions much less costly to defend (1.1.2 Defending Positions).

4. *A lack of holding power makes it more costly to maintain a position*. In slippery situations, it is difficult to hold to values, events move more quickly, resources are unreliable, connections break down, and processes vary wildly. Such positions are expensive to defend (1.1.2 Defending Positions).

5. *An abundance of holding power makes it more costly to change a position*. This is easier to understand if we think of holding power as friction, the costs of movement. Friction is a form of conflict. It affects all five elements of a position. It creates conflict among changing goals, eats up time, wears out materials, prevents people from working together, and overheats processes (3.1.3 Conflict Cost).

6. *A lack of holding power makes it less costly to change a position*. Without friction, positions are more slippery, making movement easier. This is like lubricating a machine. We can adapt our goals, save time, not get worn out, come together easily, and move processes along smoothly (3.1.3 Conflict Cost).

7. Picking the best opportunity is a simple comparison of holding power with our need for movement. While understanding opportunity holding power can seem complicated, comparisons of opportunities are usually simple. In these situations, the value of holding power depends on how long we want to hold to a given position. The more transitory a position, the less important holding power becomes. The more long-term we want to hold a position, the more important holding power becomes (1.3.1 Competitive Comparison).

Illustration:

Let us use these concepts to look at website design.

1. Holding power describes adhesion and repulsion of a potential position. In the case of website design, the nature of the opportunity depends on what we are looking for: many visitors that pass through and move on or fewer visitors that stay for a long time. Sticky websites will encourage visitors to stay. They will have longer articles, more content, and many links to that internal content. Huffington Post and YouTube are designed as sticky websites. Slippery websites will encourage visitors to move on. They will have shorter articles, less internal content, and many links to that outside content. Instapundit and Drudge are slippery websites.

2. In more stable environments, holding power appears as friction. Most websites have constantly changing content, but some websites, for example, educational organizations, will demand a certain amount of adhesion as a cost of access.

3. An abundance of holding power makes it less costly to maintain a position. Websites with good holding power will tend to maintain their audiences with less effort. Websites with less holding power must constantly change their content in order to keep attractive visitors.

4. A lack of holding power makes it more costly to maintain a position. The most common key used when cruising the web is the Back key. People visit a site and quickly return from where they came.

5. *An abundance of holding power makes it more costly to change a position*. Websites with good holding power cannot change their direction very easily. They hold their audiences but they are also held captive by the expectations of those audiences, forced to serve those expectations. Huffington Post must service a certain type of political audience, with a certain kind of story, slanted in a specific way.

6. *A lack of holding power makes it less costly to change a position*. Instapundit can post about anything that Glenn finds interesting.

7. *Picking the best opportunity is a simple comparison of holding power with need for movement*. There is a market for a range of websites, from very sticky to very slippery and through all points in between. The differences have more to do with the goals and capabilities of those who run them.

4.6 Six Benchmarks

Five key methods regarding simplifying the comparisons of opportunities.

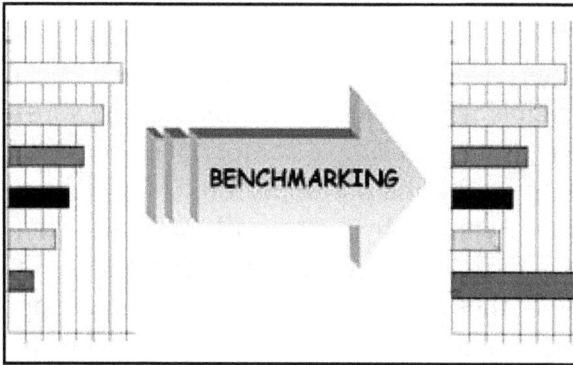

"You must be able to lead your men deeply into different surrounding territory.
And yet, you can discover the opportunity to win."
          Sun Tzu's The Art of War 11: 5:14-16

"We are all faced with a series of great opportunities brilliantly disguised as impossible situations."
          Charles R. Swindoll

General Principle: We use the six extremes in strategic space as benchmarks to evaluate future positions.

Situation:

Evaluating opportunities is one of the most sophisticated aspects of Sun Tzu's system. This is especially true given the limited amount of information we have before exploring opportunities. Twenty different key methods describe the surface characteristics of opportunities that separate good opportunities from poor ones. In the real world, we simply do not have time to compare all these characteristics rigorously. All alternative opportunities are impossible to identify. Facts and opinions vary. Most characteristics resist quantitative analysis.

Opportunity:

Fortunately, Sun Tzu offers a simple methodology. To pick the best opportunities, we use a simple mental model to help us recognize the pattern of future probabilities. These models make our decisions as simply a possible but no simpler. The yardstick that we use throughout strategy is simple comparison (1.3.1 Competitive Comparison). In evaluating our opportunities, we judge the surface characteristics we can see by benchmarking against the extremes of such characteristics (4.5 Surface Characteristics). With a general understanding of those characteristics, we can map opportunities, graphically separating high probability opportunities from low probability ones.

Key Methods:

There are no absolutes in strategy. Absolute measurements of the future are particularly impossible. By definition, decisions depending on such measures have a lot of probability of success.

1. Area, barriers, and holding power are the dimensions that measure an opportunity. Sun Tzu's strategy depends on the relative advantages in different positions. We use these three dimensions to evaluate potential positions. Thinking of these three categories as physical dimensions allows us to compare the positions of opportunities quickly and easily (4.1 Future Potential).

2. To compare area, barriers, and holding power, we only need to understand their extremes. To compare positions, we don't need exact measures. We need only to identify the **boundaries** of measurement, the extremes at both ends of the scale. From these boundaries of the minimum and maximum states, we create the simplest possible scale for comparing relative positions of opportunities (1.3.1 Competitive Comparison).

3. The extremes of area, barriers, and holding power define six benchmarks. We call these extremes the six **benchmark positions**. The method we use is to compare the potential of future competitive position against the six extreme variations of opportunities (4.5 Opportunity Surfaces).

- Spread-out positions cover a maximum of area.
- Constricted positions cover a minimum of area.
- Barricaded positions have a maximum of barriers.
- Wide-open positions have a minimum of barriers.
- Fixed positions have a maximum of holding power.
- Sensitive positions have a minimum of holding power.

4. These extremes define the potential of future positions in terms of advance and defense. The issue in pursuing an opportunity is not simply advancing a position, but defending it as well. Because all positions are paths, we have to look at how easy a given opportunity is to advance into and how easy it is to advance from (1.1 Position Paths). Spread-out positions are hard to defend and advance.

- Confined positions are easy to defend and advance.
- Barricaded positions are hard to get into and easy to defend.
- Wide-open positions are hard to defend but easy to advance.
- Fixed positions are hard to leave but easy to defend.
- Sensitive positions are easy to leave but risky to advance.

5. We compare these benchmarks not only to other opportunities but also our current position. We can see the potential and restrictions in any position by gauging it against other positions with these six benchmark positions, but even if we are not looking at other alternatives, we can compare an opportunity to our current position. The goal is just to quickly get a relative comparison. This process immediately gives us a better feeling for the possibilities of new opportunities and of our current position. We cannot see true potential and restrictions in our current position until we compare it against other alternatives against the six benchmark positions (4.2 Choosing Non-Action).

- In thinking about the amount of area an opportunity targets, is it more confined or more spread out?
- In thinking about the barriers of the target position, is it more wide-open or more barricaded?
- In thinking about the stickiness of the target positions, is it more fixed or more sensitive?

Illustration:

Let us use an illustration from sales competition, specifically, a salesperson selecting which new type of prospect to pursue. The more specific the problem, the easier these key methods are to apply, so we will make some assumptions regarding our salesperson's available options.

1. Area, barriers, and holding power are the dimensions that measure an opportunity. Since his current position is secure, he has a lot of time to invest in developing his territory, but since he plans to stay in his current market for a couple of more decades, he wants to make moves that continue to yield results for a long period of time. His biggest current problem is his inability to keep his current customers, who are easily lured away to competing products.

2. To compare area, barriers, and holding power, we only need to understand their extremes. The salesperson recognizes that there is no perfect group of customers but that the most desirable group likes at the certain extremes rather than in any mid-range. The choices are a specialized small medical market, a generic but large wide-open business market, or a market of individuals who are attracted to novelty.

3. The extremes of area, barriers, and holding power define six benchmarks. The medical market is small, requires specialized knowledge, is slow to change, and hard to contact. The generic business market is wide open, has few barriers and is relatively easy to contact. The market of individuals is in between in size, but has little holding power.

4. *These extremes define the potential of future positions in terms of advance and defense.* This medical group is easy to defend, but will require more work to win over because penetrating the market requires learning specialized knowledge so it is is protected by certain barriers. These customers tend to group together and makes changes only when required since they are hard to sell. While this market will be hard to win, it tends to stay with existing providers.

5. *We compare these benchmarks not only to other opportunities but also our current position.* The salesperson picks the medical market, not only because it is more stable than his other alternatives but because it is more dependable over the long term than his current market.

4.6.1 Spread-Out Conditions

Sun Tzu's five key methods for recognizing opportunities that are too large.

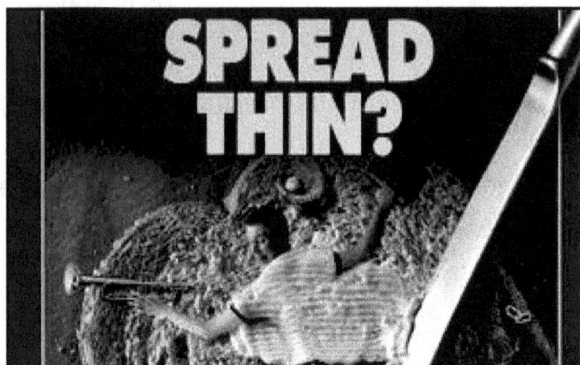

"Some field positions are too spread out."
Sun Tzu's The Art of War 10:1:45

"Perception is strong and sight weak. In strategy it is important to see distant things as if they were close and to take a distanced view of close things."
Miyamoto Musashi, *Book of Five Rings*

General Principle: Spread-out positions pull us in too many directions at once, creating strategic weakness.

Situation:

The bigger the opportunity, the more attractive it always appears, especially at a distance. Since opportunities are openings, a big opening seems to offer plenty of room with lots of potential.

Unfortunately, openings that are too large offer many more disadvantages than advantages. This raises another challenge. How do we identify opportunities that are "too large?" In comparing opportunities, we can see when one offers more area than another, but what defines "too" large?

Opportunity:

When we evaluate potential opportunities, we can easily get seduced by opportunities that are too large if we don't have a benchmark for identifying them (4.6 Six Benchmarks). We learn the distinctive characteristics of the benchmark for a maximum of area as a key point of comparison. We can then use that benchmark to identify positions that are so large that they can potentially cause problems for us.

Key Methods:

When we evaluate opportunities by their size, we recognize spread-out positions, those that are "too large" in area, by the following key methods.

1. Spread-out opportunities look like they have great potential. Most people are attracted to spreadout positions because they seem to lead to bigger and better things. They are so large that they are attractive even at a distance. Unfortunately, this mindset forgets that we are working in a competitive environment and the further that we must go, the less likely our success (4.4 Strategic Distance).

2. Spread-out positions are those that stretch our resources. Good strategy tells us to avoid spreading ourselves too thinly. Strength arises from concentrating resources. Our time is always limited. We can juggle only so many balls at a time. Add one ball too many and they all come crashing down. Spread-out regions are "too large" opportunities relative to the size of our resources to explore and develop them. They spread our limited resources too thinly across too large of a strategic area (3.1.1 Resource Limitations).

3. Spread-out positions require multiple, simultaneous points of focus. If our position pulls us in many different directions at once, we cannot defend it. Spread-out positions require us to divide our attention among many different points. Focus on a single, clear goal creates unity and strength (1.7.2 Goal Focus).

4. Spread-out positions undermine a group's unity. Problems arise occupying a position or pursuing an opportunity pulls people apart. All opportunities require some expansion, but problems arise when people are so distant from one another, physically or intellectually that they lose their unity as a team (1.7.1 Team Unity).

5. Spread-out positions are difficult to defend. Since they must be defended in multiple places at once, spread-out positions are the source of openings for others. Spread-out positions are an invitation to our opponents. Spread-out positions are weak because they invite attack. Big territories are hard to defend. They leave too many openings for our opponents to attack us (1.7 Competitive Strength).

Illustration:

Let us consider pursuing a career in music as a rock guitarist, a common mistake that wastes the talents and energy of so many young people.

1. Spread-out opportunities look like they have great potential. We see the big successes in the music business, we do not see the millions of struggling musicians.

2. Spread-out positions are those that stretch our resources. Since music does not provide enough income to support most musicians, they must pursue other careers as well, in exciting industries like fast-food service.

3. Spread out positions require multiple, simultaneous points of focus. Spreading their time between music practice, looking for gigs, trying to form a group, and working at a regular job, most musicians don't make progress on any front.

4. Spread-out positions undermine a group's unity. Music groups come together and quickly fall apart as their inability to support themselves pull members in different directions.

5. *Spread-out positions are difficult to defend.* Even when some progress is made in forming a group, developing a reputation, and getting gigs, there are always lots and lots of competitors waiting in the wings who are willing to work for less to get notoriety.

4.6.2 Constricted Conditions

Sun Tzu's five key methods for identifying and using constricted positions.

"Some field positions are constricted.
Get to these positions first."

Sun Tzu's The Art of War 10:1:33-34

"A single day is enough to make us a little larger or, another time, a little smaller."

Paul Klee

General Principle: Pick constricted opportunities over spread-out ones.

Situation:

Small opportunities are easy to miss, even when they are right in front of us. Since opportunities are openings and all openings are difficult to see, the smaller the opening the more difficult it is to see. The problem is that small opportunities always seem constricting. We need to practice seeing and embracing small opportunities because they offer many more advantages than large openings.

Opportunity:

When we evaluate potential opportunities, we need a benchmark to help us identify opportunities that are so small that they are easy to miss (4.6 Six Benchmarks). We learn the distinctive characteristics that define the minimum of area for improving our position. We can then use this benchmark to identify positions that are small but can potentially enhance our position at a minimum of cost.

Key Methods:

When we evaluate opportunities by their size, we recognize spread-out positions, those that are "too large" in area, by the following key methods.

1. Constricted opportunities look like they have little potential. Remember, opportunities are openings or needs that no one is filling. Constricted positions are so small that they can only be seen if we are close to the need they represent. Because of this, only a few people are in a position to recognize these opportunities. Unfortunately, most people miss the fact that these constricted positions actually do lead to bigger and better things. (4.4 Strategic Distance).

2. Constricted positions are those that we have more than enough resources to fill completely. We all have limited resources, but we almost always have plenty of resources to fill constricted resources. All that is required to take advantage of constricted opportunities is our commitment to them. We are only vulnerable when pursuing these opportunities if we do not commit ourselves to filling the position completely. We only have to juggle things if we have more balls than we have hands. Juggling seems exciting because failure is just a misstep away. Constricted opportunities may not seem very exciting, but we have a high-probability of successfully pursuing them. (3.1.1 Resource Limitations).

3. Constricted positions of a very narrow point of focus.
Strength arises from concentrating resources. If our position narrows our focus, we can easily win it and defend it. Constricted positions require us to focus our resources on a single small area. Focus on a single, clear goal creates unity and strength. Both are the primary sources of strategic strength (1.7.2 Goal Focus).

4. Constricted positions enhance a group's unity. We think that working closely together creates friction, but more often a group that works together closely becomes more tightly bonded. When people are physically, philosophically, and intellectually close to one another, they develop closer bonds in their unity as a team (1.7.1 Team Unity).

5. Constricted positions are easy to defend. These positions allow whoever holds them to control them naturally and easily. Niches are easy to defend because we can fill them completely, leaving no openings for others. While this is impossible if we pursue opportunities that are much larger than our resources, it is easy if we pursue opportunities that are smaller than our resources. (1.7 Competitive Strength).

Illustration:

To illustrate constricted positions, let us consider a good marriage, the most constricted and most powerful position of them all.

1. Constricted opportunities look like they have little potential.
We are told how restricting a marriage is. How old-fashioned. Men and women are both encouraged to open themselves to the wonderful world of multiple, simultaneous and sequential relationships, disposing of their current relationship whenever they feel the urge.

2. Constricted positions are those that we have more than enough resources to fill completely. No matter how limited our resources, we are endowed by our sex with unique resources that fulfill the needs of the opposite sex.

3. Constricted positions of a very narrow point of focus. In a marriage, we are focused on making our partner happy above everything else because we recognize that our happiness depends on theirs.

4. *Constricted positions enhance a group's unity.* Like any team, a man and a woman who are devoted to their marriage combine the very different but totally complementary strengths of each sex into the cause of mutual success.

5. *Constricted positions are easy to defend.* A spouse in a marriage can maintain their marriage much more easily than finding a new relationship as long as they put in the effort to maintain it.

4.6.3 Barricaded Conditions

Sun Tzu's seven key methods regarding the issues related to the extremes of obstacles.

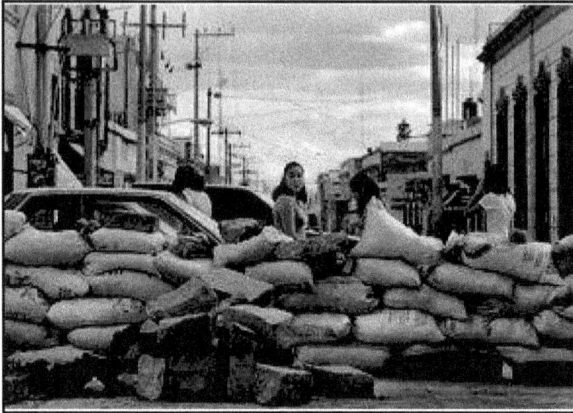

"Some field positions give you a barricade."
Sun Tzu's The Art of War 10:1:39

"If you can find a path with no obstacles, it probably doesn't lead anywhere."
Frank A. Clark

General Principle: Barricaded positions are hard to win but easy to defend.

Situation:

It is a mistake to think of barriers as a problem instead of an opportunity. When we evaluate potential opportunities, we must consider the number and types of obstacles that we will encounter in pursuing them. Obstacles are any natural characteristic that makes taking advantage of a specific opportunity difficult. Barriers to entry can be physical, but more often they are psychological and intellectual. The most common barrier to entry to any opportunity is a lack of specific knowledge.

Opportunity:

Opportunity exists as openings (3.1.4 Openings). Openings only exist when there are barriers of entry preventing them from being filled easily (4.5.2 Surface Barriers). To help us analyze the potential opportunities, we use the benchmark called barricaded positions. These are positions defined by the most extreme barriertts. We use them as a benchmark to help us understand the issues related to positions that have a maximum of barriers (4.6 Six Benchmarks).

Key Methods:

The following seven key methods define the nature of barricaded positions and how they are won.

1. Barricaded positions are the benchmark for the most barriers to entry. Competitors are blocked from getting into these positions by either physical or intellectual obstacles. Barricaded positions have a great number of obstacles, very large obstacles, or very unfamiliar obstacles. A few large barriers can be much more of an obstacle than many small barriers (4.5.2 Opportunity Barriers),

2. The more barricaded the position, the more costly it is to pursue. Barriers can only be overcome by an investment. Depending on the type of barrier, that investment can take the form of effort, time, or other strategic resources. These costs represent the initial commitment required to explore an opportunity. The less available the resources required, the less the probability that a given position will be initially profitable (3.1.2 Strategic Profitability).

3. Winning a barricaded position often requires a campaign. Campaigns are a series of moves toward a longer-term goal. The main purpose of campaigns is surmounting barriers. Familiar barriers, where the obstacles are well understood, are surmounted by repeating the steps in previous similar campaigns. Since they often require campaigns, these positions are costly and time-consuming to acquire (6.2 Campaigns).

4. The degree of cost depends on the position from which we approach the barriers. The best opportunities are those in which we find a key or angle that gives us easy entry into a barricaded position. Different types of barricades require different types of skills and resources to surmount. If we have those specific skills and resources to surmount the barricade more easily than others, we must always take advantage of the barricade (3.3 Opportunity Resources).

5. Barriers make it less costly to defend a position. While barriers decrease the initial profitability of a position, they lower the costs of maintaining a position over time. Once we are behind the barrier, the barrier protects us from would be competitors, decreasing our costs of competition. If a position is difficult to achieve when it is empty, it is invulnerable once we have filled it (3.1.3 Conflict Cost).

6. We get an advantage when we get behind the barriers first. If a barrier can be surmounted, it will be surmounted. We realize the potential of these opportunities by establishing ourselves in barricaded positions before our competitors do. Once we are in these positions, those same barriers to entry protect us (5.3.1 Speed and Quickness).

7. After winning a barricaded position, we must make it visible. Barricaded positions are often obscured by their barricades. We must be recognized for winning the value of a barricaded position. If we are seen as having a dominant position in these areas, we will win the support of others. We can only lose these positions to competitors if we abandon them.

Illustration:

A good illustration of a barricaded position is one that is protected by copyright law. For our example, let us use the example of pharmaceutical companies.

1. Barricaded positions are the benchmark for the most barriers to entry. Before any company can sell a new drug in the American market, it must navigate a series of campaigns. The drug companies know that only a small percentage of the drugs they attempt to develop will surmount the barriers involved.

2. The more barricaded the position, the more costly it is to pursue. New drugs must be researched. they must be able to protect that drug by patents so that it cannot be copied by those not paying for development. Then they must be tested to the satisfaction of the FDA in the US. The drug must go through the FDA approval process. They must be covered by insurance. They must then be marketed both to doctors and consumers.

3. Winning a barricaded position often requires a campaign. Each step in this process requires a separate strategic move. Big pharmaceutical companies, having gone through these campaigns before, have the resources necessary to complete these campaigns.

4. The degree of cost depends on the position from which we approach the barriers. Since the drug companies approach these barriers with experience in surmounting them, they are much better positioned than any doctor or scientist who discovers a new drug on their own. Over time, we developed skills in surmounting specific kinds of barrier.

5. Barriers make it less costly to defend a position. Once the drug is proven, the company developing it has it protected by patents for a certain span of time before it can be copied by generic drug makers. The length of time of protection, depends on how quickly they can negotiate the barriers involved, since patent protection starts long before the drug is proven and approved.

6. We get an advantage when we get behind the barriers first. The first drug company to develop a new drug has a certain advantage. One that develops a new category of drugs has a huge advantage.

7. After winning a barricaded position, we must make it visible. Part of the process is promoting the drug to doctors and patients. Because the barriers are temporary, they need to grow the recognition of the drug as quickly as possible.

4.6.4 Wide-Open Conditions

Six key methods regarding the issues related to an absence of barriers.

"You can attack from some positions easily.
Other forces can meet you easily as well.
We call these unobstructed positions.
These positions are open."

Sun Tzu's The Art of War 10:1:7-11

"Where there is an open mind there will always be a frontier."

Charles F. Kettering

General Principle: Establish wide-open positions quickly and make them visible.

Situation:

It is a mistake to think that the best opportunities are those that have the fewest possible barriers to entry. While obstacles make taking advantage of a specific opportunity difficult, the absence of barriers creates an opposite problem where taking advantage of an opportunity is too easy, not only for us but for everyone. Areas without barriers are highly competitive environments where it is difficult to find any competitive advantage unless we understand our situation.

Opportunity:

Opportunity exists as openings (3.1.4 Openings). This logic suggests that the most open situations would provide the most opportunities. However, wide-open positions are one of the many non-intuitive situations in strategy that require the reverse of our normal perspective (3.2.5 Dynamic Reversal). To help us analyze the potential opportunities, we use the benchmark called wide-open positions to help us understand the issues related to positions that have no barriers to entry (4.6 Six Benchmarks).

Key Methods:

The following key methods define the nature of wide-open positions and how we must handle these opportunities.

1. Wide-open positions are the benchmark for the positions with no *barriers to entry.* There are no real obstacles, physical or intellectual, preventing us or anyone else from getting into these positions. These opportunities are like fragile bubbles, protected only because people do not see them (3.2.2 Opportunity Invisibility).

2. The more open the position, the less costly it is to pursue. Barriers require an investment. Depending on the type of barrier, that investment can take the form of effort, time, or other strategic resources. These costs represent the initial commitment required to explore an opportunity. The less available the resources required, the less the probability that a given position being initially profitable (3.1.2 Strategic Profitability).

3. Winning a wide-open position requires quick, direct action. Since these opportunities have no barriers, they do not require long campaigns. The main purpose of campaigns is surmounting barriers. These positions must be established quickly, without going through a series of steps (5.3.1 Speed and Quickness).

4. We must avoid conflict in pursuing wide-open positions. As we know, conflict is always expensive. The threat of new competition tends to depress the value of this position both initially and over the longer term. Low-barrier opportunities are high-probability opportunities but they are usually low-profitability opportunities. (3.1.3 Conflict Cost).

5. We must maintain the supporters and resources we win to produce profits from these positions. As non-intuitive as it sounds, the secret to using opportunities in wide-open areas is not better competitive skills but better production skills. Maintaining existing supporters of our position is less costly than winning new supporters so we must offer as much value as we can for as little cost. More efficient forms of internal operation can make these inherently marginal positions profitable enough to justify holding them, at least for a time (1.9 Competition and Production).

6. While hard to defend, wide-open positions make good stepping stones. While the lack of barriers increases the likelihood of winning a position, they raise the costs of defending a position over time. Since there are no barriers to entry, any success we find simply attracts more competitors, decreasing the relative value of our effort by increasing our competition. Often, the main value of wide-open positions is in using them as a stepping stone to a new, less open position (3.1.2 Strategic Profitability).

7. After winning a wide-open position, we can create barriers with visibility. Wide-open positions have great visibility and lend themselves to self-promotion. We establish a position in these areas, we can create recognition for our position. Since mind space is limited even when an opportunity is wide-open, our recognition can create a more dominating position (8.3 Securing Rewards).

Illustration:

Any business that requires little training and no real capital investment defines a wide open position. So do relationships that lack any kind of commitment or investment. For our illustration, let us think about a window-washing business.

1. Wide-open positions are the benchmark for the positions with no barriers to entry. Anyone can start a business washing windows of businesses and homes.

2. The more open the position, the less costly it is to pursue. Window washing requires no investment in learning, skill development, or equipment.

3. Winning a wide-open position requires quick, direct action. Since lots of people would like their windows washed at a reasonable price, all we need to do is get out there and talk to them.

4. We must avoid conflict in pursuing wide-open positions. We cannot try to win away the customers of other window washers.

5. We must maintain the supporters and resources we win to produce profits from these positions. We must keep all existing customers, contacting them regularly to see if they need their windows cleaned again. We must get more efficient over time at both finding new customers and cleaning windows.

6. While hard to defend, wide-open positions make good stepping stones. We must look for opportunities to expand our business, into carpet cleaning or other forms of maintenance for existing customers

7. After winning a wide-open position, we can create barriers with visibility. If we get well known for providing good service, we can maintain our business.

4.6.5 Fixed Conditions

Sun Tzu's nine key methods regarding positions with extreme holding power.

"You cannot leave some positions without losing an advantage."
Sun Tzu's The Art of War 10:1:24

"For every mountain there is a miracle."
Robert H. Schuller

General Principle: Fixed positions cannot be left without losing an advantage.

Situation:

When we evaluate potential opportunities, we must consider what it means to have a great deal of holding power either in our current position or in a future position. Extreme holding power in our current position creates an unseen danger in moving on from where we are. Moving into a position with holding power offers both benefit and challenges. The biggest danger is not understanding what we are getting into. Whenever people talk about a "lack of an exit strategy," they are talking about the problems encountered in positions with extreme holding power. Sun Tzu described these conditions as "propped up," which we translated as "supporting" in the original text.

Opportunity:

We do not need an exit strategy if our current position satisfies all our needs. Our usual goal is to continually improve our position, but when life gives us the best it can offer, our opportunity is in recognizing it. Since most of us seldom reach such peaks, the value of understanding fixed positions is as benchmarks for analyzing our opportunities. We need to understand how positions with a great deal of holding power can create challenges in moving forward. We can build up these positions over time, but we cannot relinquish them without taking a step backwards. We can safely move into fixed position if we understand the permanent commitment that this position entails.

Key Methods:

The following seven key methods describe the identification of use of fixed positions.

1. Fixed positions are the benchmark for the most amount of position holding power. This holding power gives the position a great deal of permanence. In real life, some positions are much more fixed than others, but few positions are absolutely fixed for all time. We used the concept of fixed positions as a relative point of comparison, as a way of comparing positions and opportunities (4.6 Benchmarking Opportunities).

2. Fixed positions have so much holding power that we cannot move out of them. This holding power has many different affects on a position. In our Sun Tzu English translation, we translated fixed positions as "supporting" positions, for their advantages they offer. In many of our adaptations of Sun Tzu to modern competition, we use other terms, for example, *peak* positions in Golden Key to Strategy and *optimal* positions in 9 Formulas for Business Success.In The Playbook, we often reference the "stickiness" and "friction" of these holding powers (4.5.3 Opportunity Holding Power).

3. People closely identify us with our fixed position. In the intellectual aspect of positions, fixed positions are powerful because they stick in the mind. Because they stick in the mind, people gravitate toward them. Since getting mind-space is so difficult to win, this stickiness is a great advantage. One we never want to lose though it does come with cost of being "stuck" with a firmly attached label (1.2 Subobjective Positions).

4. Fixed positions are easy to defend. Since they offer many resources and are superior to all surrounding position, these positions are natural defense points. While opponents can get through barriers given enough time and resources, they cannot wear down a fixed position because it is supported by the environment, which is stronger than any competitor (3.2.1 Environmental Dominance).

5. We must carefully choose a fixed position before we are locked into it. There are many advantages in being in a fixed position, but we must be careful about making such commitments. We are going to be locked in these sticky positions for a long time, perhaps forever. We can only move out of them at a cost. The only time to consider if we want a fixed position is before we get into them. Leaving a fixed position is always costly (1.1 Position Paths)

6. Fixed positions are advanced by growth. When we are in fixed positions, we advance our position by growing it rather than by using it as a stepping stone to a new position. We extend our existing position over time, using the fixed position as an anchor point (1.8 Progress Cycle).

7. Opponents will attempt to entice us out of a fixed position. Competitors will desire our position, but they cannot win it from us. They will try to get us to abandon it. If we try to move out of fixed positions, we immediately run into problems. Even if rivals cannot take over our old position, if we let ourselves get enticed away from a fixed position, we are weakening in comparison with competitors (1.3.1 Competitive Comparison).

8. We cannot move away from fixed positions without going downhill. Fixed positions are advantageous compared to all surrounding positions. We are stuck in these because holding power offers an advantage that we cannot afford to lose. Using one physical analogy, fixed positions are like mountain peaks. They are the peak because there are no higher positions around them. However, unlike mountain peaks, we can stay on them because their "height" is the control of resources that they offer us (3.3 Opportunity Resources).

9. Fixed positions and sensitive positions can reverse over time. Positions can loose their holding powers with changes in the environment. These types of positions are the opposite extremes of holding, but, given a change in environmental conditions, these positions can follow the dynamics of reversal because of changes in the environment. Over time, a fixed position can loosen into a sensitive position and a sensitive position can get set in stone and become a fixed position (3.2.5 Dynamic Reversal).

Illustration:

The classic example of an attempt to move away from a fixed position was the attempt to change the "secret formula" of Coca-Cola with an introduction of the New Coke in 1985.

1. Fixed positions are the benchmark for the most amount of position holding power. CocaCola's secret formula had the greatest holding power in the soft drink industry.

2. Fixed positions have so much holding power that we cannot move out of them. Because of the secret recipe, Coca-Cola had built a dominating position since the drink was introduced in 1886. The recipe was changed in 1903 with the removal of the coca leaf (the source of cocaine) that was part of its original formula, but it remained unchanged since then.

3. People closely identify us with our fixed position. For many years, Coke's identity was built around their secret recipe.

4. Fixed positions are easy to defend. Coke was the "real thing." All other colas were positioned as imitators trying to duplicate the secret formula.

5. We must carefully choose a fixed position before we are locked into it. In the case of Coke, they discovered the holding power of the recipe rather than choosing it.

6. Fixed positions are advanced by growth. Coke brought out other drinks, including diet versions, but the center of their product line was always the original recipe Coke. **Opponents will attempt to entice us out of a fixed position.** Pepsi enticed Coke with their "taste challenge," which appeared to demonstrate that, without the brand awareness, people preferred Pepsi on the basis of taste alone. A classic example of using the gap between subjective and objective positions to an advantage (3.6 Leveraging Subjectivity)

7. We cannot move away from fixed positions without going downhill. Coke never tried this until 1985, when it discovered the penalties of trying to move first hand. New Coke, with a new formula, was introduced replacing original Coke in response to Pepsi's taste tests. The result was a disaster and they quickly returned to the old formula, but not without wasting a lot of resources.

8. Fixed positions and sensitive positions can reverse over time. When Coke was first introduced, its formula was not a fixed position. It's cocaine-based formula was a sensitive position that, once abandoned, could not be returned to. However, over time, the new formula became a fixed position.

4.6.6 Sensitive Conditions

Six key methods regarding the affects of positions with no holding power on pursuing opportunities.

⚠ CAUTION

SLIPPERY SLOPE

"These are entangling positions.
field positions are one-sided."
Sun Tzu's The Art of War 10:1:16-17

"All politics takes place on a slippery slope. The most
important four words in politics are 'up to a point."
George Will

General Principle: We can only advance from sensitive positions when our success is certain.

Situation:

When we are advancing our position, a lack of holding power either in our current position or in a future position can have disastrous effects. When evaluating future position, we must take these effects into account. A lack of holding power in our current positions makes moving on from where we are a one-way proposition. When moving into a position with little or no holding power, we must consider what that means to our next move. The danger in positions without holding power is not from our opponents but from losing our supporters. Whenever people talk about "getting on a slippery slope," they are talking about the dangers encountered in getting into position lacking holding power. Sun Tzu described these conditions as "hanging," which we translate as "entangling" in our translation.

Opportunity:

Since our strategic goal is to make continuous progress, we need to understand how positions can create challenges in moving forward. Sensitive positions can be valuable stepping stones if we know how to safely move into and out of them.

Key Methods:

The following key methods describe the benchmark to recognizing and dealing with positions with too little holding power.

1. Sensitive positions have no holding power. This lack of holding power has many different consequences. It means they are so slippery that we cannot return to them. Sensitive positions are loose in the sense of the opposite of fixed positions. Sun Tzu described them as entangling positions. In Golden Key to Strategy , we describe them as "one-way" positions because we cannot return to them. In 9 Formulas for Business Success , we described them as fragile positions because they are easily destroyed. The thinking behind both terms will become clear (4.5.3 Opportunity Holding Power).

2. Sensitive positions are difficult to hold onto while new positions are being established. To use a physical analogy, we usually try to advance our position like climbing a ladder. We stand on our current position, gradually transferring our weight to a better position. This works fine as long as we aren't supporting ourselves on a sensitive position. When we advance from a sensitive position, the position falls away as we take our weight off of it. We cannot return to it. Hence, it is a fragile and oneway position (1.1.2 Defending Positions),

3. Sensitive positions depend on a commitment. Even though they are slippery, we can hold onto them but only if we are completely committed to them. Sensitive positions aren't bad positions as long as we stay in them. Their weaknesses only appear in transition from them as we must eventually do (1.1 Position Paths).

4. We destroy sensitive positions when we try to move out of them. The very act of moving out of them destroys them. We cannot get back into them. If we try to advance from a sensitive position and fail to establish a new position, we cannot return to our old position (1.8 Progress Cycle).

5. Moves from sensitive positions must succeed the first time. Sensitive positions are challenging because our advance from them to a new position must succeed the first time. This means they must have the highest probability of success. If our move to a new position fails, we put ourselves exactly without a position entirely. Since our first priority is always defending our existing position until we establish a new one, we can only advance out of these positions when we are certain of our new position (5.6.1 Defense Priority).

6. Fixed positions and sensitive positions can reverse over time. These two types of positions are the opposite extremes of holding power, but, given a change in environmental conditions, these positions can follow the dynamics of reversal. Over time, a fixed position can become more sensitive and a sensitive position can get set in stone (3.2.5 Dynamic Reversal).

Illustration:

These sensitive, one-way, fragile positions are common, more common than most people think. When we quit a job or get a promotion, we usually cannot go back to our old position if our new position doesn't work out. Any position that depends largely on an exclusive relationship based on trust is a sensitive position. We have already described marriage as a constricted position because sane people limit themselves to a single spouse, but marriage is also a sensitive position.

1. Sensitive positions have no holding power. A marriage does not stick no matter what we do. If we violate our commitment, we endanger it.

2. Sensitive positions are difficult to hold onto while new positions are being established. We cannot establish a new romantic relationship and hold onto a marriage.

3. Sensitive positions depend on a commitment. Violate the commitment and the marriage falls apart.

4. We destroy sensitive positions when we try to move out of them. In almost every case, we cannot return to our spouse after a divorce.

5. Moves from sensitive positions must succeed the first time. People move to new relationships, but if those relationships do not work, they cannot go back.

6. Fixed positions and sensitive positions can reverse over time. Marriage was once a fixed position. People could not move from it without suffering desperate consequences. Because of changes in social mores, it has become a sensitive position.

4.7 Competitive Weakness

Sun Tzu's six key methods on how certain opportunities can bring out our weaknesses.

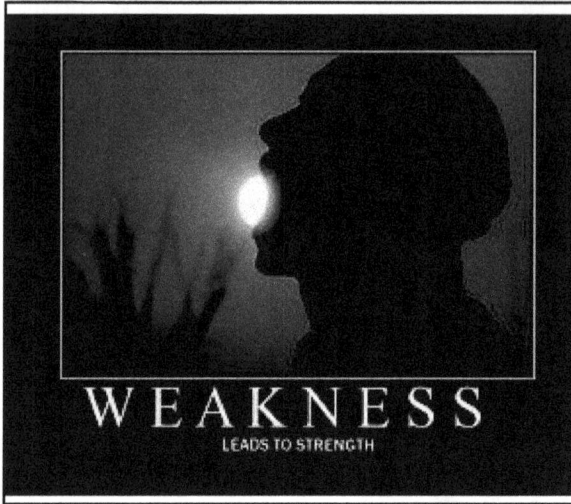

*"You must know all about these six weaknesses.
You must understand the paths that lead to defeat."*
Sun Tzu's The Art of War 10:2:31-32

"It's about human failings, human failings amplified by technology. Men are not angels. Our Constitution was written by people who understood that human nature has many flaws."

Lee Tien

General Principle: The six benchmark positions expose organizational weaknesses arising from character flaws.

Situation:

To pick the best possible opportunities, we must avoid putting ourselves in a bad position. Pursuing the wrong opportunities brings out our weaknesses. These situations fail to take advantage of our strengths. Most of us do not realize that picking the wrong opportunities can create or emphasize previously hidden weaknesses.

Opportunity:

We can see problem situations from a distance on the surface of opportunities (4.5 Surface Characteristics). We use the six benchmarks of surface characteristics to identify our potential weaknesses (4.6 Six Benchmarks). To successfully avoid the danger of moving into the wrong situations, we start with considering our fitness for a given opportunity in terms of our strengths and resources (3.4.2 Opportunity Fit). We must then consider our flaws and weakness as well. Those weaknesses arise in two areas: our character of decision-making and our organizational connection to others.

Key Methods:

We use the six benchmarks of an opportunity surface to identify potential misfits using the following key methods:

1. Weakness in a future position arises at the intersection between its nature and our fit. We think of an organization as our methods, decision-making and resources. This organization must fit the opening of an opportunity. If is docs, moving into that opening creates value. If our organization is unsuited to the nature of a space, moving into that space creates a disaster (3.4.2 Opportunity Fit).

2. The character flaws of decision-makers create organizational weakness. Weaknesses in our execution arise from flaws in our decision-making. Using elemental strategic terminology, command leadership determines group methods (1.5 Internal Elements, 1.5.2. Group Methods).

3. The five command weaknesses create six organizational weaknesses. The five command characteristics are intelligence, caring, courage, discipline, and trustworthiness. The five character flaws are the lack of these command characteristics. In interacting with others, these five flaws create organizational weakness. While these weaknesses appear in the way an organization fails at certain opportunities, the source of these problems are in the way we make decisions (4.7.1 Command Weaknesses).

4. The six opportunity benchmarks can also be used to uncover six common flaws in organizations. Few organizations lack flaws. Opportunities also have flaws as identified by the six benchmarks. Combining the wrong opportunity with the wrong organization is a disaster either in advancing into a given position or defending it. These flaws hurt every type of organization subtly in every situation.They are exaggerated in wrong form of opportunities (4.7.2 Organizational Weaknesses).

5. These flaws in a rival organization can create our opportunities. These six organizational weaknesses can affect any organization: our own or any rival. While we usually find opportunities by seeing the strength of our opponents, our examination of the surface of an opportunity can also help us identify potential traps for opponents (3.5 Strength and Weakness).

Illustration:

Taking a cue from the initial quote above, let us use the illustration of why, despite its good intentions, statism and socialism in all its forms, always fails.

1. Weakness in a future position arises at the intersection between its nature and our fit. Failed states and societies always blame their opponents and the conditions with which they must deal. They never realize that "the fault is not in our stars but in ourselves."

2. The character flaws of decision-makers create organizational weakness. This is most clearly seen in various totalitarian states because they always start as a cult of personality. The fundamental mistake is confusing the strength of unity with the strengths of a single decision-maker.

3. The five command weaknesses create six organizational weaknesses. These strong leaders imprint their excess confidence on the states that they create. The leaders condone their bad decisions by the needs of the state, but, more importantly, all their followers condone doing evil in the name of the leaders intention of creating a greater good.

4. The six opportunity benchmarks can also be used to uncover six common flaws in organizations. Totalitarian states will handle many aspects of internal control initially very well, their weaknesses always appear over time as the state must adapt to changing circumstances. This ability to adapt to the nature of emerging opportunities expose the fragility of their rigid systems regulating their citizens.

5. These flaws in a rival organization can create our opportunities. The continuous rise of totalitarian states on the Utopian promises of strong leaders lead eventually to their fall and the creation of many openings for individuals.

4.7.1 Command Weaknesses

Sun Tzu's ten key methods on the character flaws of leaders and how to exploit them.

"Know all six of these weaknesses.
They create weak timing and disastrous positions.
They all arise from the army's commander."

Sun Tzu's The Art of War 10:2:7-9

"The wise know too well their weakness to assume
infallibility; and he who knows most, knows best how
little he knows."

Thomas Jefferson

General Principle: Five character flaws are open to five forms of attack and create six organizational flaws.

Situation:

We can be poorly suited to an opportunity based on our character. An area of weak character leads to mistakes in making choices about positions. Though these mistakes appear as organizational weaknesses, they arise from character flaws. Organizations reflect those who guide them. Weakness in command leads predictably to certain types of weakness in organizations.

Opportunity:

Sun Tzu teaches that making the right strategic decisions requires intelligence, caring, courage, discipline, and trustworthiness. Each of the five areas of character relates to a specific elemental aspect of our position (1.3 Elemental Analysis). Understanding the connection between character, positions, and organizations allows us to see the opportunities that we can take advantage of better than others. We can avoid pursuing the wrong opportunities if we know ourselves and know our rivals.

Key Methods:

The following key methods describe how the five character flaws create six organizational forms of weakness.

1. A lack of intelligence leads to ignorance of the ground. The key methods work with both meanings of intelligence: our IQ and the quality of our information. Ignorance means not recognizing conditions that persist over time. In Sun Tzu's strategy, we call them "ground features." We are all ignorant about many aspects of what is changing in the future, that is climate conditions. It is a leader's absolute duty to know the nature of the ground that he and his people are moving into (1.4.2 Ground Features).

2. Ignorance of the ground leads to organizations that are outmaneuvered. When leaders fail to recognize conditions that persist over time, they cannot use the ground to their advantage and opponents can use the conditions of the ground against them. The easiest way to leverage their ignorance against them is through surprise.For example, when they do not realize where the high ground lies, opponents can secretly seize the high ground and use it to their advantage (2.1.4 Surprise).

3. The lack of caring leads to the inability to create a higher, shared mission. When we say "caring," we mean our dedication to the mission. This is almost always the result of selfishness. Selfish leaders do not remain leaders for long (1.6.1 Shared Mission).

4. Lack of a shared mission leads to self-destructive organizations that fall apart. The easiest way to leverage this weakness against leaders is through division, separating them from their supporters. The best leaders are servants of their shared mission and, through their shared mission, servants of their followers (9.2.5 Vulnerability of Organization).

5. The lack of courage means the inability to deal with climate. This means the inability to face the challenges of the future. Fear of making mistakes is normal, but leaders have to rise above it. If navigating the future were easy, people wouldn't need leaders to guide them (1.4.1 Climate Shift).

6. A inability to deal with climate leads to over-extended organizations. Over-extension arises from the fear of letting go, making decisions about what is valuable and what is not. The easiest way is use a use a lack of courage is through deception, using misinformation and disinformation to control leaders who want to play it safe (2.4.2 Climate Perspective).

7. The lack of discipline means failing in methods. This is the inability to execute on decisions. A leader who lacks discipline will make good decisions but lack of the persistence necessary to see them through difficult times (1.5.2. Group Methods).

8. Failing in methods leads to untrained and undisciplined organizations. Untrained organizations do not know what to do. Undisciplined organizations just don't do it. Strategic reflexes must be trained to keep organizations together. The easiest way to leverage a lack of discipline is by challenging it by opposing attempted moves. This is what strategy calls "battle," meeting an opponent so that they have to respond. Undisciplined leaders are unable to overcome the obstacles that confront them (6.0 Situation Response).

9. The lack of trustworthiness means losing the respect of others. Leaders must make the hard choices and they must make them correctly. As leaders, we must make our decisions quickly and clearly. If we do not make the tough decisions, followers lose trust in our leadership (1.5.1 Command Leadership).

10. The lack of clear decisions leads to disorganization. Organizations arise out of the leader taking responsibility and followers accepting the leader's decision. Where decisions are sloppy, lazy, and unclear, there is no organization. The best way to oppose untrustworthy leaders is simply challenging them for their position. This is called siege. If people are untrustworthy, they leave themselves open to being replaced in their responsibilities (2.4.3 Command Perspective).

Illustration:

We will need a variety of examples from a variety of competitive domains to illustrate all these failures.

1. A lack of intelligence leads to ignorance of the ground. When Time/Warner bought AOL, they didn't understand the nature of the internet and the world wide web.

2. Ignorance of the ground leads to organizations that are outmaneuvered. The AOL environment that Time/Warner had hoped to use to deliver paid content was soon outdated by the free content on the broader Internet.

3. The lack of caring leads to the inability to create a higher, shared mission. In organizations such as the UN, the bureaucrats that rise to the top are more focused on their personal careers than any solid philosophy.

4. Lack of a shared mission leads to self-destructive organizations that fall apart. Because its various members put their self-interest above everything, the organization is useless in terms of action against countries such as Iran.

5. *The lack of courage means the inability to deal with climate*. As overseas cars became more popular, US car makers needed the courage to identify a position that they could defend instead of drifting into a more difficult future.

6. *A inability to deal with climate leads to over-extended organizations*. Instead, companies such as GM and Ford all bought overseas car companies, such as Saab and Jaguar. Eventually, they had to sell them off.

7. *The lack of discipline means failing in methods*. Dell rose to become the largest computer manufacturer due to their innovative sales of computes over the web. However, their organization's quick success never allowed them to develop solid operating methods.

8. *Failing in methods leads to untrained and undisciplined organizations*. Operational problems in support (Dell Hell) and questions about financial irregularities started to erode people's trust in the organization.

9. *The lack of trustworthiness means losing the respect of others*. We are seeing this problem demonstrated right now with President Obama's administration. People on the right and left are quickly losing trust in the administration's direction and commitment.

10. *The lack of clear decisions leads to disorganization.* The inability of the Democrats to pass legislation despite huge majorities in each house of Congress is due entirely to the lack of organization.

4.7.2 Group Weaknesses

Sun Tzu's six key methods regarding organizational weakness and where they fail.

"You must know all about these six weaknesses. You must understand the philosophies that lead to defeat."

Sun Tzu's The Art of War 10:2:31-32

"There are two kinds of weakness, that which breaks and that which bends."

James Russell

General Rule: The six benchmark positions expose six common forms of organizational weaknesses.

Situation:

Flaws in leaders lead to flaws in organizations. All organizations are flawed in some way, but the flaws in organizations become fatal when we put them in inappropriate situations. A weak organization is one that pursues the wrong opportunities. We must avoid putting our organizations in a bad position. We cannot put our group in the wrong place at the wrong time by pursuing those opportunities that highlight the groups weaknesses.

Opportunity:

Five weaknesses in character leads to six forms of organizational weakness (4.7.1 Command Weaknesses). These six forms of organizational weakness can be matched against the six benchmarks that are used to analyze opportunities (4.6 Six Benchmarks). From this process, we can know which opportunities are most likely to create serious problems for a given organization. An objective appraisal of our opportunities relative to our particular group is a huge advantage. We can avoid these weaknesses before pursuing the wrong opportunities.

Key Methods:

These are six key methods describing the six weaknesses of groups and the ground that exposes them:

1. Spread-out positions expose overextended organizations. Overextended organizations are already trying to do more than they can do well, failing to expect competition. Their leaders want more ground than they realistically can control. The spread-out position is often chosen by overextended organizations. More focused competitors are usually stronger in specific areas. By spreading too few resources over too much ground, overextended organizations cannot defend their position at any point of attack and are forced to retreat (4.6.1 Spread-Out Positions).

2. Confined positions expose self-destructive organizations. Self-destructive organizations suffer from a lack of mission. Their leaders let each group develop its own separate goals and priorities. In Sun Tzu's strategy, unity is strength. The advantage of confined regions is that they are easy to defend, physical closeness is not unity. If the organization is not united, it falls apart. Without a clear, uniting mission, people follow their own personal goals. These enterprises will self-destruct over time, especially on confined ground where everyone must work together closely (4.6.2 Constricted Positions).

3. Barricaded positions expose disorganized organizations. Disorganized organizations take their eye off of the ball. The safety of a barricaded position allows their leadership to grow overconfident and fall out of touch with the changes of climate. Relying on the natural barriers to competition, these organizations lack direction and gradually decay over time. Such negligence is quickly punished in most positions, waking people up to what is changing, but in barricaded positions, negligence grows and grows leading to chaos (4.6.3 Barricaded Positions).

4. Wide-open positions expose clumsy organizations. Clumsy organizations cannot adapt to the moves that their rivals make because they don't understand the ground. They have the most difficulty in wide-open positions that have few barriers to entry. Like spread-out positions, wide-open positions invite competition. Competitors must act and react quickly to use this position. In a wide-open position, clumsy organizations are too slow are easily outmaneuvered by competitors (4.6.4 WideOpen Positions).

5. Fixed positions expose untrained organizations. Untrained organizations consist of people who have failed to learn proven methods. This weakness occurs in stable, fixed positions, where leaders take their positions for granted, failing to emphasize training and hiring trained people. In these organizations, good decisions are wasted because they cannot be executed. Since fixed positions are usually optimal positions in a competitive arena, the usually result is that these organizations fall down from their peaks (4.6.5 Fixed Positions).

6. Sensitive positions expose undisciplined organizations. Undisciplined organizations suffer from leadership that is too lax. These organization are most vulnerable in sensitive positions where execution must be precisely controlled. Sensitive positions do not forgive bad decisions.

7. Organizations get entangled in sensitive positions, naturally slipping out of them into weaker positions and unable to return to them. Sensitive positions rely on great decisions about when to defend these positions and when to move from them (4.6.6 Sensitive Positions).

Illustration:

We will continue with a variety of illustrations that parallel those given in 4.7.1 Command Weaknesses :

1. Spread-out positions expose overextended organizations. American car companies, specifically GM, is a great example.

2. Confined positions expose self-destructive organizations. The example is the UN, which fails whenever it has to focus with a specific situation in the world.

3. Barricaded positions expose disorganized organizations. President Obama's administration is a good example.

4. Wide-open positions expose clumsy organizations. Time/Warners' movement into the Internet with the acquisition of AOL is a classic example.

5. Fixed positions expose untrained organizations. Coke's introduction of New Coke is the classic example.

6. Sensitive positions expose undisciplined organizations. Dell's losing its leading position in computer sales is a good example.

4.8 Climate Support

Sun Tzu's eight key methods to help us choose new positions based on future changes.

"Don't attack into the wind."
Sun Tzu's The Art of War 12:2:14

"When in doubt, predict that the present trend will continue."
Merkin's Maxim, Murphy's Laws

General Rule: Choose opportunities that are built up by trends in climate.

Situation:

To make the best decisions about pursuing opportunities, we not only have to consider current conditions but the direction in which those positions are likely to change. So far we have looked at future positions from their more static (ground) conditions of distance, form, surface, and fit. Now we need to think about future positions from the perspective of how those positions are going to be naturally built up or eroded by the current trends.

Opportunity:

Success requires adapting to the environment not trying to control it (3.2.1 Environmental Dominance). Our positions are advanced in two ways: by what we choose to do and by what the environment does naturally on its own (1.1.1 Position Dynamics). In the first case, we use time and effort ro move to better and better positions like stepping stones (1.1 Position Paths). In the second case, we stay in a position because the trends in that environment are naturally moving that position up. By choosing the right positions, we can use them like escalators, improving our position effortlessly.

Key Methods:

The following key methods describe the use of trends in picking the best opportunities.

1. We must not only identify trends but identify how long those trends are going to last. Of course, it takes strategic skills to identify positions that are going up and effort to move into them. Most strategic mistakes are mistakes of timing: abandoning trends just as they are about to catch on or, much more common, jumping on a trend just as it is about to change. People are naturally skeptical of trends. Most people don't necessarily buy into them until everyone else does. However, by definition, once *everyone* buys into a trend, the trend is over because there is no one else left to buy into it (7.4 Timing).

2. When a trend goes too far, we must prepare for it to naturally reverse itself. In Sun Tzu's strategy, we have a clear explanation for this phenomena. We think about trends of change as being driven by the competing forces that we call complementary opposites (3.2.3 Complementary Opposites). These forces create a balance. To understand opportunity, we think about this balance in terms of emptiness and fullness. Emptiness is the opening that defines opportunities. Fullness is the crowded state that leads to costly conflict (3.2.5 Dynamic Reversal).

3. *A trend measures the movement of people from emptiness to fullness.* As people start to move to a new open position, a trend begins. This movement supports the people that got to that position first, improving their position as the crowd comes in behind them (3.2.4 Emptiness and Fullness).

4. *At some point, the new opening gets over-crowded.* The good ground is taken. The opportunities are fewer. People stop coming in and those who are there start to leave. Depending on the nature of the ground, they either go back to where they were before, or go onto some other new territory that has just been opened up (3.1.4 Openings).

5. *Success depends totally on how we use the trend.* If we were one of the first to a new opening, we are going to do very well. However, if we come in later, after the needs have been filled, our efforts in competition with those who were there first and have deeper knowledge cannot be profitable (2.6 Knowledge Leverage).

6. *When we are in the middle of a trend, it always looks like it is going to last forever.* It never does. The more popular a trend becomes, the closer it is to reversing itself (3.1.6 Time Limitations).

7. *We can guess on the lifespan of an opportunity by its surface characteristics.* The strategic tools for determining how long a trend will last, whether it is at the beginning or end of the trend, are the same three dimensions that we have been using for picking the best opportunities (4.5 Surface Characteristics):

- **The larger the ground for the trend, the longer the trend will last.** The more people that are potentially involved, the more people that can potentially jump on board, The smaller the area, the fewer people it affects, the shorter it will last.
- **The more barriers there are, the slower the trend will develop and the longer it will last.** Trends that go suddenly straight up in one direction are suspect. The rate of increase cannot be sustained.

- **The more holding power a trend has, the longer it will last.** The combination of memorability and deep appeal that make up holding power is the most difficult dimension to quantify but we can see their affects over time. The longer trends have lasted the more likely they are to continue to last.

8. Move when a trend shows signs of exhausting itself. Good strategy starts with accepting that neither we nor anyone else can know trends for certain. In our journey, we are going to make mistakes. We are going to choose positions that are going up and going down. We have to be willing to adapt through our movements to what is actually happening. Both long trend and short trend can be used to support a position. We can always move to a new position as a trend exhausts itself, but to do so we must have some feel for the length of trends to use the best timing (1.8.2 The Adaptive Loop).

Illustration:

Let us look at the trend in the markets driving up the price of gold.

1. We must not only identify trends but identify how long those trends are going to last. If we are going to invest in gold, we have to know if that investment is long or short-term.

2. When a trend goes too far, we must prepare for it to naturally reverses itself. While gold has been going up since the dollar was disconnected from it, at some point in the future, the price of gold will start to decline in price, at least temporarily, because it is over-bought. When there are no more buyers, the price must decline.

3. A trend measures the movement of people from emptiness to fullness. Think of the "boom towns." When gold was discovered, people flooded into an area. In the case of the price of gold today, people are not so much moving into gold as moving away from paper money, fiat money. As long as there are more people who begin to think that printed money is less solid than gold, gold will continue to go up.

4. At some point, the new opening gets over-crowded. At some point, everyone who is going to invest in gold will have invested. They will start to move to other types of value.

5. Success depends totally on how we use the trend. Money can be made when the price of gold goes up or down depending on whether we go long or short.

6. When we are in the middle of a trend, it always looks like it is going to last forever. Since this is a very long-term trend, starting in the 1930s, it looks like it will continue forever.

7. We can guess on the lifespan of an opportunity by its surface characteristics.

- **The larger the ground of the trend, the longer the trend will last.** There are a lot of people in the world, such as the Chinese, that are just getting the opportunity to buy gold. Many others, because of recent financial crises, are growing less trusting in paper money.
- **The more barriers there are, the slower the trend will develop and the longer it will last.** In the past, there were many restrictions and physical difficulties in buying gold. Most of those have gone away, which is why gold has been going up more quickly. The only barriers left are psychological: other investments are seen as more rational.
- **The more holding power a trend has, the longer it will last.** Gold has had value for most of human history.

8. Move when a trend shows signs of exhausting itself. At the time this was written, the price of gold had risen quickly. These price increases must sustain themselves. These will be corrections. In a given week, the price of gold can decline by 5%. The big question at any point remains: what do people trust more: currency, stocks and bonds, or gold? The fact that gold is appearing on that list for the first time tells us something about the times.

4.9 Opportunity Mapping

Five key methods regarding a two-dimensional tool for comparing opportunities probabilities.

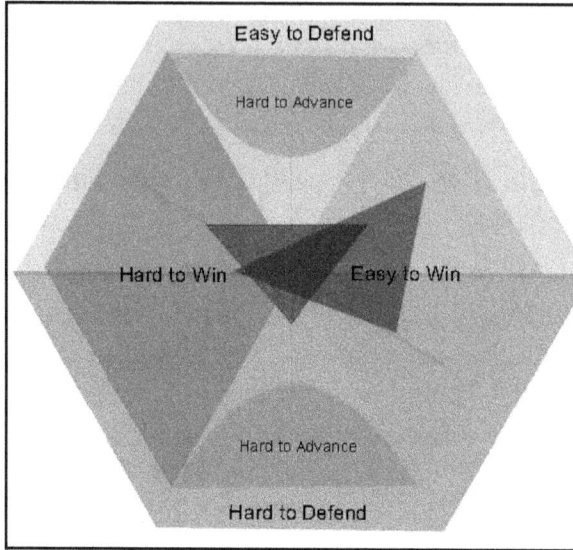

"You can recognize the opportunity for victory; you don't create it."

Sun Tzu's The Art of War 4:1:10

"A good map is both a useful tool and a magic carpet to far away places."

Anon

General Rule: Graphically mapping opportunities using the six extremes of surface characteristics makes their potential easier to see.

Situation:

Sun Tzu's three dimensions—distance, barriers, and dangers—that describe opportunities and their six extremes provide a lot of information to consider in evaluating opportunities. As humans, we tend to consider one or two things that jump out at us rather than the complete picture. When our methods are purely conceptual, we miss many of our best opportunities because we cannot "see" the key characteristics of the opportunity involved.

Opportunity:

We are wired primarily for visual perception. A simple way to identify the best opportunities is by mapping them according to the six benchmarks (4.6 Six Benchmarks). We can use a mapping tool that we call the Opportunity Map. The Opportunity Map is a visual tool to see the relative advantages and disadvantages of various opportunities. The Opportunity Map provides a two-dimensional representation of the three dimensions (area/barriers/holding power) used to identify the highest probability opportunities.

Key Methods:

The Opportunity Map is a training tool, used to practice comparing opportunities. The key methods for using the hexagon of the Opportunity Map as a tool for visualizing the relative merits of different opportunities are as follows.

1. The Opportunity Map *is a hexagon showing the six bench marks as extremes on three axes.* The line between each of the benchmarks represents a range. The area range is between the extremes of confined and spread-out areas. The barrier range is between barricaded and wide-open areas. The holding power range is between fixed and sensitive or sticky and slippery areas, if that works better. (4.6 Six Benchmarks).

2. We can evaluate our current position or a future opportunity by where we think it falls on each scale. We do this simply by marking where we think that opportunity falls on each of these three ranges. Is it more barricaded or open, confined or spread-out, fixed or sensitive. *See example below.*

3. We then connect the three marks to create a triangle. This triangle represents where the position sits on the Opportunity Map.

4. We then replace the six benchmarks map with the characteristic map. This map breaks the hexagon into five regions. The regions show how difficult the position will be to win, defend, and advance. The triangle will overlap several areas, but it will fall more into some than others. The higher it is, the easier it is to defend. The more to the right is, the easier it is to win. The more centered it is, the easier it is to advance. High probabilities are easy to win, defend, and advance.

5. By mapping several opportunities, we can easily compare where they fall. Obviously, we are looking for opportunities that are more in the upper, right section where positions are easier to win and defend.

Illustration:

We will illustrate the key methods above through actual illustrations.

1. The Opportunity Map **is a hexagon showing the six bench marks as extremes on three axes.** The value of these benchmarks is that they are not exact measures, but simply comparisons of positions between two extremes. *See example below.*

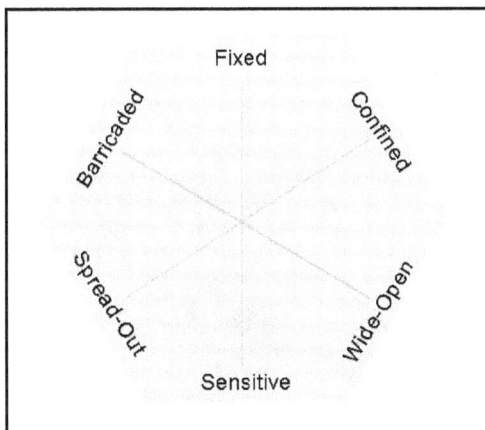

2. *We can evaluate our current position or a future opportunity by where we think it falls on each scale.* In this case, we see this opportunity as more barricaded than open, more confined than spread-out, and perhaps a little more sensitive. *See example below.*

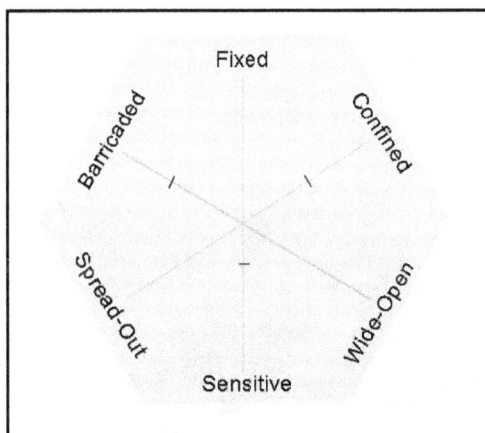

3. *We then connect the three marks to create a triangle.* How large the triangle is doesn't matter, just where it falls in the hexagon. *We then replace the six benchmarks map with the characteristic map.* The first opportunity we charted above falls mostly in the

easy to defend region, but it is split evenly between easy and hard to win. *See example below.*

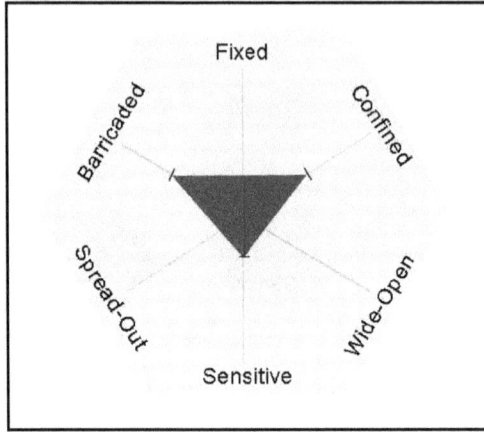

4. By mapping several opportunities, we can easily compare where they fall. In comparing the first opportunity with a second, we can see that both are easier to defend but the second opportunity is much easier to win. This makes the second opportunity a better choice. *See example below.*

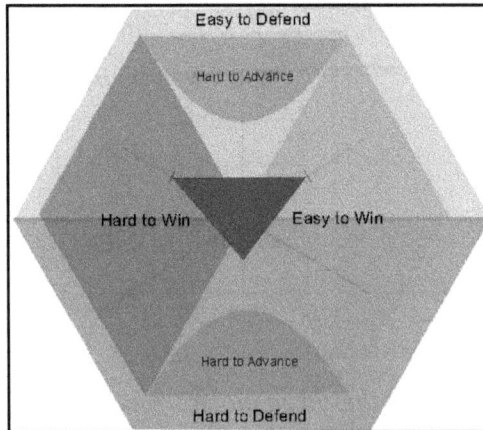

5.

6. By mapping several opportunities, we can easily compare where they fall. The area covered by the triangles show their relative advantages. *See example below.*

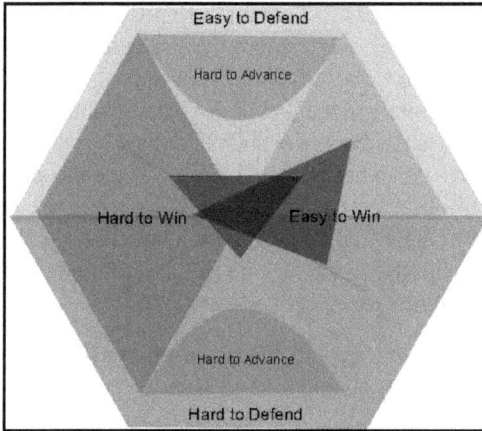

Glossary of Key Concepts from
Sun Tzu's *The Art of War*

This glossary is keyed to the most common English words used in the translation of *The Art of War*. Those terms only capture the strategic concepts generally. Though translated as English nouns, verbs, adverbs, or adjectives, the Chinese characters on which they are based are totally conceptual, not parts of speech. For example, the character for conflict is translated as the noun "conflict," as the verb "fight," and as the adjective "disputed." Ancient written Chinese was a conceptual language, not a spoken one. More like mathematical terms, these concepts are primarily defined by the strict structure of their relationships with other concepts. The Chinese names shown in parentheses with the characters are primarily based on Pinyin, but we occasionally use Cantonese terms to make each term unique.

Advance (*Jeun* 進): to move into new **ground**; to expand your **position**; to move forward in a campaign; the opposite of **flee**.

Advantage, *benefit* (*Li* 利): an opportunity arising from having a better **position** relative to an **enemy**; an opening left by an **enemy**; a **strength** that matches against an **enemy's weakness**; where fullness meets emptiness; a desirable characteristic of a strategic **position**.

Aim, *vision, foresee* (*Jian* 見): **focus** on a specific **advantage**, opening, or opportunity; predicting movements of an **enemy**; a skill of a **leader** in observing **climate**.

Analysis, *plan* (*Gai* 計): a comparison of relative **position**; the examination of the five factors that define a strategic **position**; a combination of **knowledge** and **vision**; the ability to see through **deception**.

Army: see **war.**

Attack, *invade* (*Gong* 攻): a movement to new **ground**; advancing a strategic **position**; action against an **enemy** in the sense of moving into his **ground**; opposite of **defend**; does not necessarily mean **conflict**.

Bad, *ruined* (*Pi* 圮): a condition of the **ground** that makes **advance** difficult; destroyed; terrain that is broken and difficult to traverse; one of the nine situations or types of terrain.

Barricaded: see **obstacles.**

Battle (*Zhan* 戰): to challenge; to engage an **enemy**; generically, to meet a challenge; to choose a confrontation with an **enemy** at a specific time and place; to focus all your resources on a task; to establish superiority in a **position**; to challenge an **enemy** to increase **chaos**; that which is **controlled** by **surprise**; one of the four forms of **attack**; the response to a **desperate situation**; character meaning was originally "big meeting," though later took on the meaning "big weapon"; not necessarily conflict.

Bravery, *courage* (*Yong* 勇): the ability to face difficult choices; the character quality that deals with the changes of **CLIMATE;** courage of conviction; willingness to act on vision; one of the six characteristics of a leader.

Break, *broken, divided* (*Po* 破): to **divide** what is **complete**; the absence of a **uniting philosophy**; the opposite of <u>unity</u>.

Calculate, *count* (*Shu* 數): mathematical comparison of quantities and qualities; a measurement of **distance** or troop size.

Change, *transform* (*Bian* 變): transition from one **condition** to another; the ability to adapt to different situations; a natural characteristic of **climate**.

Chaos, *disorder* (*Juan* 亂): **conditions** that cannot be **foreseen**; the natural state of confusion arising from **battle**; one of six weaknesses of an organization; the opposite of **control**.

Claim, *position, form* (*Xing* 形): to use the **ground**; a shape or specific condition of **ground**; the **ground** that you **control**; to use the benefits of the **ground**; the formations of troops; one of the four key skills in making progress.

Climate, *heaven* (*Tian* 天): the passage of time; the realm of uncontrollable **change**; divine providence; the weather; trends that **change** over time; generally, the future; what one must **aim** at in the future; one of five key factors in **analysis;** the opposite of **ground**.

Command (*Ling* 令): to order or the act of ordering subordinates; the decisions of a **leader**; the creation of **methods**.

Competition: see <u>war.</u>

Complete: see <u>unity.</u>

Condition: see **ground.**

Confined, *surround* (*Wei* 圍): to encircle; a **situation** or **stage** in which your options are limited; the proper tactic for dealing with an **enemy** that is ten times smaller; to seal off a smaller **enemy**; the characteristic of a **stage** in which a larger **force** can be attacked by a smaller one; one of nine **situations** or **stages**.

Conflict, *fight* (*Zheng* 爭): to contend; to dispute; direct confrontation of arms with an **enemy**; highly desirable **ground** that creates disputes; one of nine types of **ground,** terrain, or stages.

Constricted, *narrow* (*Ai* 狹): a confined space or niche; one of six field positions; the limited extreme of the dimension distance; the opposite of **spread-out**.

Control, *govern* (*Chi* 治): to manage situations; to overcome **disorder**; the opposite of **chaos**.

Dangerous: see **serious.**

Dangers, *adverse* (Ak 阨): a condition that makes it difficult to **advance**; one of three dimensions used to evaluate advantages; the dimension with the extreme field **positions** of **entangling** and **supporting**.

Death, *desperate* (Si 死): to end or the end of life or efforts; an extreme situation in which the only option is **battle**; one of nine **stages** or types of **terrain**; one of five types of **spies**; opposite of **survive**.

Deception, *bluffing*, *illusion* (Gui 詭): to control perceptions; to control information; to mislead an **enemy**; an attack on an opponent's **aim**; the characteristic of war that confuses perceptions.

Defend (Shou 守): to guard or to hold a **ground**; to remain in a **position**; the opposite of **attack**.

Detour (Yu 迂): the indirect or unsuspected path to a **position**; the more difficult path to **advantage**; the route that is not **direct**.

Direct, *straight* (Jik 直): a straight or obvious path to a goal; opposite of **detour**.

Distance, *distant* (Yuan 遠): the space separating **ground**; to be remote from the current location; to occupy **positions** that are not close to one another; one of six field positions; one of the three dimensions for evaluating opportunities; the emptiness of space.

Divide, *separate* (Fen 分): to break apart a larger force; to separate from a larger group; the opposite of **join** and **focus**.

Double agent, *reverse* (Fan 反): to turn around in direction; to change a situation; to switch a person's allegiance; one of five types of spies.

Easy, *light* (Qing 輕): to require little effort; a **situation** that requires little effort; one of nine **stages** or types of terrain; opposite of **serious**.

Emotion, *feeling* (Xin 心): an unthinking reaction to **aim**, a necessary element to inspire **moves**; a component of esprit de corps; never a sufficient cause for **attack**.

Enemy, *competitor* (Dik 敵): one who makes the same **claim**; one with a similar **goal**; one with whom comparisons of capabilities are made.

Entangling, *hanging* (Gua 懸): a **position** that cannot be returned to; any **condition** that leaves no easy place to go; one of six field positions.

Evade, *avoid* (Bi 避): the tactic used by small competitors when facing large opponents.

Fall apart, *collapse* (Beng 崩): to fail to execute good decisions; to fail to use a **constricted position**; one of six weaknesses of an organization.

Fall down, *sink* (Haam 陷): to fail to make good decisions; to **move** from a **supporting position**; one of six weaknesses of organizations.

Feelings, *affection, love* (*Ching* 情): the bonds of relationship; the result of a shared **philosophy**; requires management.

Fight, *struggle* (Dou 鬥): to engage in **conflict**; to face difficulties.

Fire (*Huo* 火): an environmental weapon; a universal analogy for all weapons.

Flee, *retreat, northward* (*Bei* 北) :to abandon a **position**; to surrender **ground**; one of six weaknesses of an **army**; opposite of **advance**.

Focus, *concentrate* (*Zhuan* 專): to bring resources together at a given time; to **unite** forces for a purpose; an attribute of having a shared **philosophy**; the opposite of *divide*.

Force (*Lei* 力): power in the simplest sense; a **group** of people bound by **unity** and **focus**; the relative balance of **strength** in opposition to **weakness**.

Foresee: see **aim**.

Fullness: see **strength**.

General: see **leader**.

Goal: see **philosophy**.

Ground, *situation, stage* (*Di* 地): the earth; a specific place; a specific condition; the place one competes; the prize of competition; one of five key factors in competitive analysis; the opposite of **climate**.

Groups, *troops* (*Dui* 隊): a number of people united under a shared **philosophy**; human resources of an organization; one of the five targets of fire attacks.

Inside, *internal* (*Nei* 內): within a **territory** or organization; an insider; one of five types of spies; opposite of *Wai*, outside.

Intersecting, *highway* (*Qu* 衢): a **situation** or **ground** that allows you to **join**; one of nine types of terrain.

Join (*Hap* 合): to unite; to make allies; to create a larger **force**; opposite of **divide**.

Knowledge, *listening* (*Zhi*: 知): to have information; the result of listening; the first step in advancing a **position**; the basis of strategy.

Lax, *loosen* (*Shii* 弛): too easygoing; lacking discipline; one of six weaknesses of an army.

Leader, *general, commander* (*Jiang* 將):
the decision-maker in a competitive unit; one who **listens** and **aims**; one who manages **troops**; superior of officers and men; one of the five key factors in analysis; the conceptual opposite of *fa*, the established methods, which do not require decisions.

Learn, *compare* (*Xiao* 效): to evaluate the relative qualities of **enemies**.

Listen, *obey* (*Ting* 聽): to gather **knowledge**; part of **analysis**.

Listening: see **knowledge**.

Local, *countryside* (*Xiang* 鄉): the nearby **ground**; to have **knowledge** of a specific **ground**; one of five types of **spies**.

Marsh (*Ze* 澤): **ground** where footing is unstable; one of the four types of **ground**; analogy for uncertain situations.

Method: see **system**.

Mission: see **philosophy**.

Momentum, *influence* (*Shi* 勢): the **force** created by **surprise** set up by **standards**; used with **timing**.

Mountains, *hill, peak* (*Shan* 山):uneven **ground**; one of four types of **ground**; an analogy for all unequal **situations**.

Move, *march, act* (*Hang* 行): action toward a position or goal; used as a near synonym for <u>dong</u>, act.

Nation (*Guo* 國): the state; the productive part of an organization; the seat of political power; the entity that controls an **army** or competitive part of the organization.

Obstacles, *barricaded* (*Xian* 險): to have barriers; one of the three characteristics of the **ground**; one of six field positions; as a field position, opposite of **unobstructed**.

Open, *meeting, crossing* (*Jiao* 來): to share the same **ground** without conflict; to come together; a **situation** that encourages a race; one of nine **terrains** or **stages**.

Opportunity: see <u>advantage.</u>

Outmaneuver (*Sou* 走): to go astray; to be **forced** into a **weak position**; one of six weaknesses of an army.

Outside, *external* (*Wai* 外): not within a **territory** or **army**; one who has a different perspective; one who offers an objective view; opposite of **internal**.

Philosophy, *mission, goals* (*Tao* 道): the shared **goals** that **unite** an **army**; a system of thought; a shared viewpoint; literally "the way"; a way to work together; one of the five key factors in **analysis**.

Plateau (*Liu* 陸): a type of **ground** without defects; an analogy for any equal, solid, and certain **situation**; the best place for competition; one of the four types of **ground**.

Resources, *provisions* (*Liang* 糧): necessary supplies, most commonly food; one of the five targets of fire attacks.

Restraint: see **timing.**

Reward, *treasure, money* (*Bao* 賞): profit; wealth; the necessary compensation for competition; a necessary ingredient for **victory; victory** must pay.

Scatter, *dissipating* (*San* 攸): to disperse; to lose **unity;** the pursuit of separate **goals** as opposed to a central **mission;** a situation that causes a **force** to scatter; one of nine conditions or types of terrain.

Serious, *heavy* (*Chong* 重): any task requiring effort and skill; a **situation** where resources are running low when you are deeply committed to a campaign or heavily invested in a project; a situation where opposition within an organization mounts; one of nine **stages** or types of **terrain.**

Siege (*Gong Cheng* 攻城): to move against entrenched positions; any movement against an **enemy's strength;** literally "strike city"; one of the four forms of attack; the least desirable form of attack.

Situation: see **ground.**

Speed, *hurry* (Sai 馳): to **move** over **ground** quickly; the ability to **advance positions** in a minimum of time; needed to take advantage of a window of opportunity.

Spread-out, *wide* (*Guang* 廣): a surplus of **distance;** one of the six **ground positions;** opposite of **constricted.**

Spy, *conduit, go-between* (*Gaan* 間): a source of information; a channel of communication; literally, an "opening between."

Stage: see **ground.**

Standard, *proper, correct* (*Jang* 正): the expected behavior; the standard approach; proven methods; the opposite of surprise; together with **surprise** creates **momentum.**

Storehouse, *house* (*Ku* 庫): a place where resources are stockpiled; one of the five targets for fire attacks.

Stores, *accumulate, savings* (*Ji* 糧):resources that have been stored; any type of inventory; one of the five targets of fire attacks.

Strength, *fullness, satisfaction* (*Sat* 實): wealth or abundance or resources; the state of being crowded; the opposite of Xu, empty.

Supply wagons, *transport* (*Zi* 輜): the movement of **resources** through **distance;** one of the five targets of fire attacks.

Support, *supporting* (*Zhii* 支): to prop up; to enhance; a **ground position** that you cannot leave without losing **strength;** one of six field positions; the opposite extreme of gua, entangling.

Surprise, *unusual, strange* (*Qi* 奇) : the unexpected; the innovative; the opposite of **standard**; together with **standards** creates **momentum**.

Surround: see **confined.**

Survive, *live, birth* (*Shaang* 生): the state of being created, started, or beginning; the state of living or surviving; a temporary condition of fullness; one of five types of spies; the opposite of **death.**

System, *method* (*Fa* 法): a set of procedures; a group of techniques; steps to accomplish a **goal**; one of the five key factors in analysis; the realm of groups who must follow procedures; the opposite of the **leader.**

Territory, *terrain*: see **ground.**

Timing, *restraint* (*Jie* 節): to withhold action until the proper time; to release tension; a companion concept to **momentum.**

Troops: see **group.**

Unity, *whole, oneness* (*Yi* 一): the characteristic of a **group** that shares a **philosophy**; the lowest number; a **group** that acts as a unit; the opposite of **divided.**

Unobstructed, *expert* (*Tong* 通): without obstacles or barriers; **ground** that allows easy movement; open to new ideas; one of six field positions; opposite of **obstructed.**

Victory, *win, winning* (*Sing* 勝): success in an endeavor; getting a reward; serving your mission; an event that produces more than it consumes; to make a profit.

War, *competition, army* (Bing 兵): a dynamic situation in which **positions** can be won or lost; a contest in which a **reward** can be won; the conditions under which the principles of strategy work.

Water, *river* (*Shui* 水): a fast-changing **ground**; fluid **conditions**; one of four types of **ground**; an analogy for change.

Weakness, *emptiness, need* (*Xu* 虛): the absence of people or resources; devoid of **force**; the point of **attack** for an **advantage**; a characteristic of **ground** that enables **speed**; poor; the opposite of strength.

Win, *winning*: see **victory.**

Wind, *fashion, custom* (*Feng* 風): the pressure of environmental forces.

The *Art of War Playbook* Series

There are over two-hundred and thirty articles on Sun Tzu's competitive principles in the nine volumes of the *Art of War Playbook*. Each volume covers a specific area of Sun Tzu strategy.

About the Translator and Author

Gary Gagliardi is recognized as America's leading expert on Sun Tzu's *The Art of War*. An award-winning author and business strategist, his many books on Sun Tzu's strategy have been translated around the world. He has appeared on hundreds of talk shows nationwide, providing strategic insight on the breaking news. He has trained decision makers from some of the world's most successful organizations in competitive thinking. His workshops convert Sun Tzu's many principles into a series of practical tools for handling common competitive challenges.

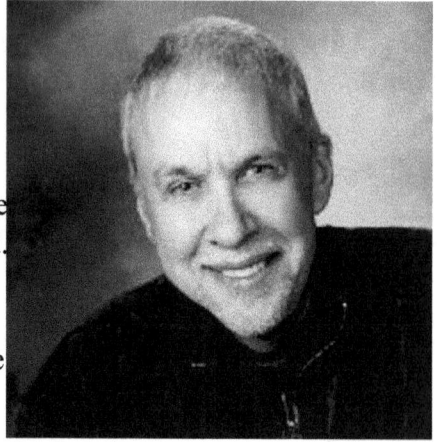

Gary began using Sun Tzu's competitive principles in a successful corporate career and when he started his own software company. In 1990, he wrote his first *Art of War* adaptation for his company's salespeople. By 1992, his company was on *Inc. Magazine's* list of the 500 fastest-growing privately held companies in America. He personally won the U.S. Chamber of Commerce Blue Chip Quality Award and was an Ernst and Young Entrepreneur of the Year finalist. His customers—AT&T, GE, and Motorola, among others—began inviting him to speak at their conferences. After becoming a multimillionaire when he sold his software company in 1997, he continued teaching *The Art of War* around the world.

Gary has authored several breakthrough works on *The Art of War*. Ten of his books on strategy have won book award recognition in nine different non-fiction categories.

Art of War Books by Gary Gagliardi

www.ingramcontent.com/pod-product-compliance
Lightning Source LLC
Chambersburg PA
CBHW050124210326
41519CB00015BA/4099